FIVE HABITS OF HIGH-IMPACT SCHOOL BOARDS

Doug Eadie

Published in partnership with the
National School Boards Association

Rowman & Littlefield Education
Lanham • New York • Toronto • Oxford

Published in partnership with the
National School Boards Association

This title was originally published by ScarecrowEducation.
First Rowman & Littlefield Education edition 2006.

Published in the United States of America
by Rowman & Littlefield Education
A Division of Rowman & Littlefield Publishers, Inc.
A wholly owned subsidiary of The Rowman & Littlefield Publishing Group, Inc.
4501 Forbes Boulevard, Suite 200, Lanham, Maryland 20706
www.rowmaneducation.com

PO Box 317
Oxford
OX2 9RU, UK

Copyright © 2005 by Doug Eadie

British Library Cataloguing in Publication Information Available

Library of Congress Cataloging-in-Publication Data
Eadie, Douglas C.
  Five habits of high-impact school boards / Doug Eadie.
      p. cm.
  "Published in partnership with the National School Boards Association."
  ISBN 1-57886-176-4 (pbk. : alk. paper)
  1. School boards—United States. I. Title.
LB2831.E34 2005
379.1'531—dc22

                                                        2004011726

⊗™ The paper used in this publication meets the minimum requirements of
American National Standard for Information Sciences—Permanence of Paper
for Printed Library Materials, ANSI/NISO Z39.48-1992.
Manufactured in the United States of America.

To my mother,
Ina Mae Crawford Eadie,
1915–2003.
Her flame ever burned brightly.

CONTENTS

FOREWORD

When we see a public school system succeeding on all important fronts—in terms of student achievement, parental involvement, administrative efficiency, financial stability, and strong public support—we can be sure its school board is hard at work providing the high-impact leadership that these turbulent times demand.

Of course, many factors determine a district's effectiveness in carrying out its educational mission, but none is more important than a school board that is realizing its full potential as a governing body and making a real difference in district affairs—in close partnership with the district's superintendent and senior administrators. We are, therefore, delighted that the National School Boards Association (NSBA) has joined with ScarecrowEducation in publishing Doug Eadie's *Five Habits of High-Impact School Boards*. This short but thought-provoking book is a concrete manifestation of NSBA's strong commitment to providing our nation's 14,890 or so public school boards with the tools they need to govern effectively.

School board members who want to take their leadership to the next level will find *Five Habits of High-Impact School Boards* an indispensable guidebook. Drawing on his twenty-five years of experience working with almost five hundred public and nonprofit organizations, including many public school systems, Doug Eadie has provided practical, tested wisdom you can put to good use in building your board's governing capacity. We believe you'll appreciate Doug's perspective on the nuts-and-bolts governing work school boards must do to make a real difference in their districts, as well as his close attention to the unique needs and circumstances of school board members. His model of proactive, creative board involvement in developing agreement on the district's core values and mission, building and maintaining the board–superintendent team, and encouraging parent involvement and community engagement is congruent with NSBA's Key Work of School Boards, a framework of eight key action areas that support and guide school boards as they focus their efforts on student achievement.

Five Habits of High-Impact School Boards is not only a reservoir of useful ideas but also a quick and enjoyable read; it's a conceptually powerful work that is at the same time unpretentious and down to earth. You'll want to keep your copy as a ready reference and reliable roadmap as you take the next steps in your governing journey.

George H. McShan
President
National School Boards Association

PREFACE

THE TRILOGY AT A GLANCE

Five Habits of High-Impact School Boards is the third book in a trilogy aimed at providing school board members, superintendents, and senior administrators with very practical, down-to-earth, thoroughly tested guidance that can be put to immediate use in building both a board's capacity to do truly high-impact governing and a board–superintendent partnership that is close, productive, and enduring. All three books in the trilogy eschew fancy theorizing, offering instead plain-spoken counsel based on real-life experience in working with hundreds of public and nonprofit boards and CEOs, including many school boards and superintendents.

The first two books in the trilogy, which speak most directly to superintendents and senior administrators, are joint publications of the American Association of School Administrators (AASA) and ScarecrowEducation. In the first book in the series, *The Board-Savvy Superintendent*, my coauthor, Paul Houston, AASA's CEO, and I describe the attitudes and executive skills critical to "board savvyness" and take a close look at steps superintendents can take to build their boards' capacity to do high-impact governing. *The Board-Savvy Superintendent* devotes considerable attention to the "gold standard" for board involvement in planning: leading strategic innovation and change.

The second book in the trilogy, *Eight Keys to an Extraordinary Board–Superintendent Partnership*, is essentially a team-building manual. It describes very practical, well-tested approaches that superintendents and senior administrators can employ in building and maintaining a partnership with their school boards that is capable of generating the strong leadership these challenging times demand while also withstanding inevitable stresses and strains. *Eight Keys to an Extraordinary Board–Superintendent Partnership* focuses heavily on the psychological and emotional dimension of this very precious but always fragile partnership, dealing with such questions as how to build board members' feelings of ownership for their governing work and how to make their governing work more interesting and enjoyable.

EXPLICITLY FOR SCHOOL BOARD MEMBERS

Although certain broad themes and key concepts weave a common thread among the three books in this governance trilogy, this third book, a joint publication of the National School Boards Association and ScarecrowEducation, speaks directly to the thousands of volunteers serving on school boards in the United States. *Five Habits of High-Impact School Boards* is written from the unique perspective of school board members who lead and serve districts of all sizes—urban, suburban, and rural. It responds to questions and concerns raised countless times over the years in hundreds of retreats that I have facilitated and educational programs that I have presented. It is intended to be an easily accessible, down-to-earth guidebook, providing succinct, to-the-point information that school board members and their superintendents can put to immediate, practical use in their districts to generate the high-impact governing decisions these changing, challenging times demand.

AN EXTRAORDINARILY IMPORTANT MATTER

Building the capacity of your school board to do high-impact governing work should be one of your highest priorities. The need for strong school board leadership has never in our history been greater. Granted, even in the best of times, leading and administering public school districts has never been a piece of cake. People have always been reluctant to tax themselves to finance their schools; teachers have never been paid at a level commensurate with the importance of their contribution to economic and social well-being; there have always been ample numbers of citizens with axes to grind where the schools are concerned; and we have always tended to have unrealistic expectations about what our schools can accomplish beyond the educational basics.

Although there has never been an educational golden age in this country that can qualify as the valid object of our nostalgic yearning, I think it's fair to say that the challenges facing public education today are unprecedented, calling for the leadership of truly high-impact school boards capable of making a significant difference in the affairs of their districts. High on the list of challenges that school board members must grapple with these days is No Child Left Behind (NCLB), which is not only a concrete manifestation of growing (and quite valid) public concern over student achievement but also an enormous expansion of federal involvement in public education at the local level. In lieu of significantly greater federal funding, many school districts will be hard pressed to meet mandated performance standards as measured by standardized testing.

But NCLB is only one of a number of challenges facing school boards around the country. Steadily increasing numbers of single parents and the dramatic growth in two-career marriages have exacted a serious toll in terms of parental involvement in children's lives. Simplistic notions of competition in the educational "marketplace" threaten to further erode school funding while also depriving struggling schools of their better students, making performance improvement an extraordinary challenge. Single-issue ax grinders appear ever more strident in pursuing their parochial interests no matter what collateral damage they are apt to cause. The list could go on, but the point is that school boards today must provide the strongest possible leadership if their districts are to accomplish their educational missions fully and cost-effectively.

However, despite the tremendous need for school board leadership of the highest order, the sad fact is that many school boards are not capable of the kind of high-impact governing work that will make a real difference in their districts. They fall so short of their governing potential that, in my professional opinion, school boards, along with other public and nonprofit boards, might very well be America's most underdeveloped and underexploited precious asset. This dismal situation is clearly not the result of an inadequate pool of people who are bright and committed enough to govern at a high level. Rather, it reflects inadequate attention to developing and managing our school boards as governing organizations, which is what *Five Habits of High-Impact School Boards* is all about.

SIX KEY ASSUMPTIONS

Six guiding assumptions undergird the practical guidance you will find in *Five Habits of High-Impact School Boards*:

1. *Governing is a noble profession.*
    With few exceptions, school board members are not paid much, if anything, for their commitment of time and energy to leading their districts. Their governing service is part of a proud American, quasi-religious tradition of volunteering in the interest of the wider good of the community and society. Never in American history have so many citizens devoted so much time to volunteer effort, and many see board service—rightly in my opinion—as the capstone of a volunteer "career," offering the greatest opportunity to make a positive difference in the world around them.

2. *High-impact governing makes a huge difference.*
    High-impact governing boards make a huge difference in their school districts, significantly affecting their districts' financial stability, educational quality, student achievement, executive leadership, and public relations. A high-impact governing board achieves powerful leadership results by focusing board time and attention on the judgments and decisions that involve the highest stakes for its district: its values and vision, its strategic goals for long-range district development, its revenue generation strategies, its operational performance targets, its annual budget, and more.

3. *High-impact governing boards must be developed.*
    High-impact governing boards are made, not born; serious governing work that makes a significant impact in a school district is

highly complex and difficult to do well. It certainly involves far more than merely thumbing through staff-produced documents as part of old-time policy making. Experience has taught that building your school board's capacity to do high-impact governing work requires consciously and systematically developing your board as an organization: developing its composition, its detailed governing role, its detailed governing functions and processes, and its governing structure.

4. *The superintendent must be an active partner in board capacity building.*

   Your school board cannot possibly go it alone in building its capacity to do high-impact governing. Board members' typically demanding lives outside the board severely limit the time they can devote even to becoming knowledgeable about the subject of board leadership. It is totally unrealistic to expect school board members to be experts in governance or to take the lead in developing their governing capacity. Behind every truly high-impact school board is a "board-savvy" superintendent who views helping his or her board develop its governing capacity as a top priority. Rather than sit back bemoaning deficiencies in board performance, board-savvy superintendents devote substantial time and attention to keeping up with advances in the rapidly changing field of public and nonprofit governance and take the initiative in getting their boards involved in building their capacity to do high-impact governing work.

5. *High-impact boards must own their governing work.*

   Ownership is a powerful force in leadership; feelings of ownership fuel commitment and enable us to weather tough times. School boards become the owners of their governing work by, first, playing an active role in developing themselves as governing organizations—helping to flesh out their governing functions, processes, and structure. Second, school board members' feelings of ownership are strengthened when they play a proactive role in shaping the governing "products" they make judgments and decisions about (e.g., an updated district values and vision statement), rather than merely thumbing through finished staff documents.

6. *High-impact school boards must do more than govern.*

Although your preeminent responsibility as a school board member is to make high-impact governing judgments and decisions, high-impact boards also play an active role in maintaining relationships with the wider public and key stakeholders in your community. There is really no choice, in light of the tremendous importance of your district's image and its relationships with key constituents to your district's well-being, on the one hand, and the unique resources that school board members bring to the public relations arena. This critical symbolic and political role includes helping to shape your district's desired image (which might be tailored to particular stakeholders in the community), attending district functions, speaking in appropriate forums on behalf of your district, participating in media programs, and serving as liaison with key stakeholder groups.

THE FIVE HABITS

My work with hundreds of public and nonprofit boards, including many school boards, over the past 25 years has taught me that school boards that make a significant difference in the affairs of their districts by doing truly high-impact governing share five key behavioral traits. These are the five habits that make up this book:

Habit 1: High-impact school boards concentrate on governing above all else.

These boards understand their governing work, map out their governing functions in detail, and devote the bulk of their time to carrying out their governing responsibilities. This does not mean that school board members should avoid doing such nongoverning work as representing their districts in an economic development summit meeting convened by the chamber of commerce. But it does mean that governing is always put first, and nongoverning work is not allowed to dilute the board's governing performance.

Habit 2: High-impact school boards develop their capacity to govern.

To ensure they are able to carry out their high-impact governing work in a full and timely fashion, high-impact school boards play a creative, in-depth role in developing their members as a human resource, updating their organizational design, meticulously managing their performance as a governing body, and fostering teamwork on the board. Of course, school boards cannot—and should not—go it alone in developing their governing capacity; they must work collaboratively with their superintendents and executive managers.

Habit 3: High-impact school boards play an active role in leading innovation and change.

In today's constantly changing, always challenging, and frequently threatening world, effectively leading and managing district innovation and change is a preeminent key to district success over the long run. School board members are uniquely qualified to participate creatively and proactively in identifying strategic issues and setting innovation and change targets to address them. High-impact school boards treat leading change as the "gold standard" for board involvement in district affairs. In doing so, they are employing a powerful new tool that is rapidly supplanting traditional long-range planning: the strategic change portfolio approach.

Habit 4: High-impact school boards pay close attention to the board–superintendent partnership.

School boards that make a real difference in their districts always work in close partnership with their superintendents, but this most precious of partnerships is also notoriously fragile and requires constant, close attention to prevent erosion. Negotiating superintendent-specific leadership targets and regularly evaluating superintendent performance against these negotiated targets is the preeminent tool for keeping the relationship healthy.

Habit 5: High-impact school boards reach out externally and internally.

Even though high-impact school boards concentrate above all else on their governing responsibilities, they also play an active, leading role in reaching out to key constituencies in their communities and internally within the school system. This role—which school board members are uniquely equipped to play—includes both governing and nongoverning work: updating your district's desired image; tailoring that image to particular high-priority stakeholder groups and organizations; fashioning strategies to promote the image and to build effective relationships with stakeholders; and engaging in such hands-on activity as speaking on behalf of your district in appropriate community forums, appearing at official school functions, and visiting classrooms in your district.

NOT INTENDED TO BE A FULL MEAL

The "chewable bites" of wisdom that make up *Five Habits of High-Impact School Boards* are not intended to sate your appetite for solid, detailed information on high-impact governing work and on the board–superintendent partnership. Indeed, I hope that your appetite is whetted by reading this book. *Five Habits of High-Impact School Boards* will point you in the right directions and get you thinking about the right questions, but I strongly recommend that you build a comprehensive library and systematically build your knowledge and expertise in the complex, rapidly changing field of public and nonprofit governance. Meanwhile, you might want to dip into the first two books in this trilogy as a practical and immediate way to expand your knowledge of K–12 governance.

ACKNOWLEDGMENTS

I am indebted to the thousands of public and nonprofit board members and CEOs, including many school boards and superintendents, who have provided me the opportunity to thoroughly test and refine the key concepts in this book. Without the opportunity to do hands-on work with so many client organizations over the past quarter century, I would have necessarily written a much more theoretical—and far less useful—book. I am also in the debt of the two national associations that copublished this and the earlier two books in my trilogy on the school board–superintendent partnership: the National School Boards Association (NSBA), headed by its executive director, Anne Bryant, and the American Association of School Administrators (AASA), whose executive director, Paul Houston, coauthored the first book in the trilogy with me.

Both NSBA and AASA have sponsored a number of my educational workshops, at which I presented the key concepts in this book and discussed them with hundreds of school board members and superintendents. Senior executives in both associations have also generously shared their wise counsel on school governance, and in this regard I want to acknowledge the following: at NSBA, Dick Anderson, Katrina Kelley,

Adria Thomas, Joe Villani, Kanisha Williams-Jones, and Sally Zakariya; at AASA, Joe Cirasuolo, Christopher Daw, Jay Goldman, C. J. Reid, and Judy Seltz.

Many state associations have also sponsored my educational programs, thereby providing me with further opportunity to interact with—and learn from—educational leaders around the country. I deeply appreciate the support I have received from the Association of California School Administrators; the Buckeye Association of School Administrators; the Colorado Association of School Executives; the Cooperative Council of Oklahoma School Administrators; the Indiana Association of Public School Superintendents; the Kansas Association of School Administrators; the Michigan Association of School Boards; the Minnesota Association of School Administrators; the Montana School Boards Association; and the School Administrators of Iowa.

As was true of the first two books in this trilogy, *Five Habits of High-Impact School Boards* has benefited from the insightful counsel and strong support of Tom Koerner, senior vice president and editorial director at ScarecrowEducation, and Cindy Tursman, ScarecrowEducation's managing editor.

This book is dedicated to my mother, Ina Mae Crawford Eadie, who died in November 2003, as this manuscript was nearing completion. There is much of Mother in this and my other two books in this trilogy on the school board–superintendent partnership. She enrolled in a nearby college in the mid-1950s, when she was in her early 40s and five of her six children were still at home in the little Illinois town where I grew up. A first-generation college graduate, Mother became a dedicated, highly accomplished special English teacher, making a tremendous difference in the lives of her hundreds of students in Illinois, Idaho, and Oregon. Mother inspired in all of us six siblings a deep respect for public education, and her passion for the noble profession of teaching certainly influenced me, helping to make writing this book a labor of love.

My 25 years of work in the public and nonprofit governance field have taught me that family and work must be creatively integrated if one is to fully realize his or her natural potential in life. In this regard, I am indebted to my best friend, professional colleague, and wife, Barbara Carlson Krai, without whose love, friendship, and strong encouragement I could not have managed to write this book while also managing a thriving consulting practice. And the emotional "line of credit" I have drawn on in my writing has been enriched and continuously replenished by my children, Jenny and Will; my stepchildren, Steve, Donna, Sean, and Kevin; and now my four grandchildren, Lane, Savannah, Thomas, and Padric.

Of course, I am totally responsible for any shortcomings you might find in this book.

❶

HABIT 1:
CONCENTRATE ON GOVERNING

A PROUD TRADITION

As a school board member, you are part of a large and amazingly diverse extended family of public and nonprofit governing bodies that are responsible for leading some 2.5 million institutions and organizations engaged in providing essential services in such sectors as education, health care, social services, economic and community development, the fine and performing arts, and more. If you are typical of the hundreds of school board members I have met over the past quarter century, you sincerely believe that high-quality citizen-owned and -led public education is one of the cornerstones of our democratic society, and you take very seriously the obligation to serve your community through your school board service. Indeed, school board service is part of a grand philanthropic tradition in America whose enduring strength can be seen in the millions of volunteer hours devoted to governing nonprofit and public organizations and institutions of all shapes and sizes.

You join an estimated thirty million largely unpaid volunteers who regularly contribute their precious time and energy to the wider public good through their public and nonprofit board service. Whether the members of these boards are elected, self-appointed, or selected by a third party such as the mayor or board of county commissioners, they participate in an American rite of passage: reaching the point in life where giving back to the community or profession becomes a compelling interest. Altruism is alive and well in these United States!

REALIZING A POWERFUL RETURN

As you have perhaps learned by this time in your school board career, governing a school district is a complex, time-consuming, and frequently stressful and frustrating job that can be exhausting even when everything is going smoothly and you are not immersed in dealing with one crisis or another. You find yourself constantly working your way through a stack of paper that is regularly replenished, you spend countless hours in meetings, you must deal with often-angry constituents, and every now and then you face a real crisis that demands extraordinary time and energy and probably ample pain and suffering as well. And for the great majority of school board members in the United States, this incredibly demanding job pays little if anything.

Giving some serious thought to the return on investment (ROI) that you can validly expect from your extraordinarily demanding governing labors need not be at the expense of altruism. In fact, thinking through the ROI that you should realize from your investment of time and energy in governing your school district is likely to make you more effective at governing, as well as replenish your always draining reservoir of emotional energy. In my experience, "burned out" school board members tend to give, give, and give more without receiving enough in return, until they grind to a halt—exhausted, unsatisfied, and often depressed. Perhaps for some there is something about being a martyr to a just cause that provides perverse satisfaction, but for most it just plain feels like failure, and eventually they burn out.

So, what nonmonetary ROI can you validly expect from all your governing effort? Long experience has taught me that the preeminent key to school board member satisfaction is playing a creative and proactive role in doing truly high-impact governing work that makes a significant difference in district affairs, primarily as measured by improved student performance, and that fully capitalizes on board members as a precious asset. This should be the very least to expect from your labors in the boardroom.

And keep in mind that your board's achievement of this level of governing performance depends more than anything else on the conscious and systematic development of the board as a governing organization.

GOVERNING WORK IN A NUTSHELL

Over the past 25 years I have interviewed thousands of board members in preparation for planning retreats and educational programs. One question I always ask is, "In a nutshell, what makes up the governing work of your board?" More often than not the initial reaction is stunned silence, which after a minute or so is typically followed by the observation that governing is "policy making." Without question, fashioning and adopting policies is part of your school board's governing work, but if you reflect on the fact that a policy is basically a broad rule to govern one aspect or another of your district's operations, you can see that, strictly speaking, making policies could not possibly keep a self-respecting board very busy.

In the first place, not many policies are important enough to merit your school board's attention (such as promotion standards, graduation requirements, suspension criteria); most relate to administrative matters that shouldn't even show up on your board's radar. In the second place, once a set of policies is in place, keeping them updated is not that big a deal, involving occasional peaks of activity when a major policy (e.g., the compensation structure of your district) demands comprehensive re-working but by no means a steady stream of governing work. So if fashioning policies is such a small part of your school board's governing work, what exactly does it mean "to govern"?

My definition, which is based on my observation of the real-life work of nearly five hundred public and nonprofit boards, is that governing means

your school board's playing the leading role, in partnership with your superintendent and senior administrators, in making decisions and judgments that answer—over and over again as part of a neverending drama—three fundamental questions that actually determine the shape and direction of your school district: (1) Where should our school district be headed over the long run? (the strategic planning question); (2) What should our school district be now and in the short run? (the operational planning question); and (3) How well is our school district performing—educationally, financially, administratively? (the monitoring question).

A high-impact school board is, very simply, one that carries out its governing role—according to the foregoing definition—in a full and timely fashion.

TRAVELING THE BOARD DEVELOPMENT ROAD

What all governing bodies, including your school board, have in common is that they are basically organizational units within their wider organizations: a formally constituted, relatively permanent group of people working through formal structure and process to achieve a common mission. Of course, the primary mission of your school board is to govern your public school organization, and one of the preeminent characteristics of high-impact school boards that make a significant difference in the affairs of their districts is that they make governing their highest priority. However, just because your school board concentrates on governing your district does not mean that board members cannot validly participate in important nongoverning activities, such as attending graduation ceremonies and speaking on behalf of your district at the monthly Rotary or chamber of commerce meeting. But it does mean that you and your board colleagues will not let nongoverning activities dilute your fundamental governing mission.

Like any other organizational entity in your school district—such as the office of the superintendent and the finance, curriculum and instruction, and buildings and grounds departments—your school board can be developed with an eye to making it more effective at carrying out its governing work, thereby enhancing its governing impact in your district. Or, of course, you and your board colleagues can merely inherit the board of the past, relying on governing practices developed by your predecessors. If you choose to be an active participant in developing your board, you can employ various approaches to turning your board into a higher-impact governing body: mapping out its governing role and functions more clearly and in greater detail; improving the processes it employs in carrying out its governing role (e.g., how it participates in strategic and operational planning and budget preparation); developing the structure it employs to facilitate its governing work (e.g., board standing committees); and strengthening the board as a human resource (e.g., by implementing a governing skills development program).

SAD TO SAY

Many school boards in the United States fall short of realizing their full governing potential in practice, depriving their districts of sorely needed leadership and their members of the satisfaction that participation in serious governing work can provide. The basic reason for their failure to perform at peak capacity as governing bodies, in my experience, is that these boards are seriously underdeveloped and undermanaged as organizations. Indeed, if our school districts paid the same attention to developing and managing their finance departments that they pay to developing their boards, financial chaos would be epidemic in districts throughout the country.

You would think that developing the school board as an organization—building its capacity to govern—would be a top priority in every school district in the United States, commanding close, sustained attention. After all, school boards, like all other governing bodies, reside at the pinnacle of the organizational pyramid, taking responsibility for such complex and demanding work as setting long-range directions, making strategic decisions, and fashioning critical policies to guide district operations. Sad to say, however, board organizational development has traditionally not been a high priority in any sector.

The price of failing to develop your board as a governing organization can be quite high, in terms of both inadequate board leadership and of board member dissatisfaction and frustration. In hundreds of interviews with board members over the years, I have heard over and over again the following lament: "I feel such a gap between my life outside of the board, where I get lots of satisfaction, and my life as a board member, which is so frustrating and unsatisfying. In my business, I really know what I am doing, but I don't really have a clear idea of what governing is all about. I sure thumb through a mountain of documents, and I'm as busy as the law allows, but I'm not certain that I'm making much of a difference."

One reason that systematic board development is still a rarity is that, until fairly recently, the detailed "business" of governing has received surprisingly little attention in the literature and in graduate education, despite the valiant efforts of the National School Boards Association and other organizations dedicated to building more effective boards. If you doubt this, check out the books on boards at any major bookstore; I guarantee that you will find very few and probably none on public and nonprofit boards. Even today, you will find few really thorough graduate courses on governance in schools of education, business, nonprofit management, and public administration. I frequently speak at K–12 conferences of administrators and school board members, and I always ask who in the audience has taken a comprehensive course in graduate school on the work of the school board. Only a few hands are ever raised, and I saw not one upraised hand at a recent presentation to some five hundred assembled school executives in the upper Midwest.

I am not certain why governance generally and board organizational development more specifically have received so little attention until recently, but my guess is that the inattention is the result of two factors. First, since school boards consist of laypersons who are not for the most part professionals in the educational enterprise, governing has been seen as an amateur undertaking that does not deserve serious study. Second, several generations of school administrators have, in the process of advancing through the ranks, acquired a fundamentally defensive attitude toward school boards, seeing them as a damage control challenge rather than as a precious asset to be developed. Defensive educational administrators tend to think of board development narrowly—in terms of establishing clear boundaries to protect themselves and their administrative colleagues from board incursions into the administrative realm.

I encountered this kind of defensiveness early in my career some 25 years ago, when I was discussing board leadership with the superintendent of a large, affluent suburban district. When I asked him what he was doing to help his board play a more creative and proactive role in shaping the annual operational plan and budget of the district, the answer was a blank stare. Probing a bit more, I obviously ruffled his feathers a bit, prompting him to declare that "the budget is my responsibility as the top administrator and not something I want the board dabbling in." He went on to say, "My job is to produce a top-quality document; theirs is to review it, making any changes they want, and ultimately to adopt it," adding that he "had no intention of opening Pandora's box by getting the board more involved than it always had been." End of story—and, of course, of any chance of turning this board into a really high-impact governing body.

Whatever the reasons for the traditional underdevelopment of school boards as organizations, meeting today's tremendous governing challenges requires that school board members and superintendents begin to work closely together in developing their boards' capacity to govern. And you have every right to expect that you will spend your time as a school board member doing well-defined governing work through well-developed governing processes.

DEVELOPING YOUR GOVERNING WORK IN DETAIL

The organizational development process of a board naturally begins by looking at the content of governing work. You will recall that earlier in this chapter I defined your board's governing role generally as playing a leading role in answering three fundamental questions over and over again: Where should our school district be headed over the long run? What should our school district be now and in the short run? How well is our school district performing? Taking this definition as a starting point, you can readily see that the governing work your school board must do to answer the three fundamental governing questions can be broken down into particular judgments and decisions about concrete governing "products." For example, in answering the first question— Where should our school district be headed over the long run?—high-impact boards make decisions about such critical products as the district's vision for the future; the district's long-range or strategic goals; strategic change initiatives that the district has launched to deal with major issues; and its long-range capital improvements and construction plan. Answering this fundamental question also involves the appointment of a new superintendent whenever a vacancy occurs.

With regard to the second fundamental question—What should our school district be now and in the short run?—high-impact boards make decisions about such critical planning products as the district's mission statement; its annual operating plan and budget; and policies to govern the district's operations. Answering this question also involves reaching agreement with the superintendent on his or her executive leadership targets for the coming year, above and beyond the districtwide operating plan.

With regard to the third fundamental governing question—How well is our school district performing?—high-impact boards make judgments, based on examining performance reports, about the district's performance in the areas of education, finance, internal administration, and external relations. Answering this key governing question also involves the board's annual evaluation of superintendent performance as CEO of its district.

COLLABORATIVE PROCESS DESIGN

It is a no-brainer that you and your colleagues on the board would not want to get involved in *doing* the detailed educational and administrative work of running your district. The thought of board members participating in the detailed development of curricula, the preparation of class schedules, the evaluation of classroom performance, or other comparable operational functions would send cold chills up and down any self-respecting superintendent's spine. School board members meddling in the detailed operations of a school district would signal maximum feasible dysfunction! School boards are rightly expected to focus more on ends than means, on setting directions and fashioning policies rather than putting them into operation. This is what was meant by the old saying, "Boards make policy, administrators carry it out."

But when you move into the governing "business" in your district, attempting to draw a solid line separating the governing work of your school board from the work of the superintendent and top administrators would not make any sense. The fact is, governing is shared turf, and doing truly high-impact governing work requires that your board, superintendent, and top administrators work as a close-knit strategic leadership team. In practice, this means that the members of your district's strategic leadership team collaborate in ongoing process design, going through the following key steps:

- Reaching agreement on the key governing decisions and judgments that regularly need to be made (e.g., adopting the annual budget)
- Working out the steps involved in getting to the key decisions (e.g., holding a special operational planning work session to discuss major operating targets for your district's budget units as a key step in budget preparation)
- Determining where it makes sense in the process for your school board to be involved and the nature of that involvement (e.g., merely reviewing a staff-prepared document of some kind or playing a more active role in shaping a particular document)

A CLOSER LOOK AT GOVERNING PROCESS DESIGN

If this sounds a bit like opening Pandora's box, throwing a tremendous amount of very complex governing work up for grabs, and risking chaos, be assured that mapping out the work that your board, superintendent, and top administrators should do in dealing with particular governing decisions can be handled incrementally, as a process more of fine-tuning than one-fell-swoop reform. Nor is your district faced with coming up with the answers from scratch; your board and superintendent can draw on the experience of numerous high-impact governing boards, as reported, for example, in this and the earlier two books in the trilogy. The point is to go beyond merely inheriting past practice, giving serious thought to the governing decisions your school board should be making and the processes that should be employed to make sure the decisions are made in a full and timely fashion, and to map out the roles and responsibilities of board members, the superintendent, and senior administrators in carrying out specific steps in the process of getting to the decision point.

Designing the processes involved in doing governing work can be simplified by dividing the work into three broad streams that encompass the great majority of board governing judgments and decisions:

- Building and maintaining the board–superintendent partnership
- Making strategic and operational planning decisions
- Monitoring district performance

For example, you can easily envision the executive, or governance, committee of your school board spending 3 hours in an intensive work session with your superintendent, reaching agreement on his or her CEO-specific leadership targets for the coming year (e.g., devoting substantial time to rebuilding the district's working relationship with the office of the mayor). You can see how your board's planning committee could reach agreement with your superintendent on the key planning products that your board should pay attention to year after year (e.g., an updated vision statement or a set of operational priorities); the major events in your district's annual planning calendar; and the respective roles of the board, superintendent, and senior administrators in bringing off each of these events.

And it is not much of a stretch to envision your board's operational oversight committee reaching agreement with your superintendent and chief financial officer on the format and content of the financial reports that will be sent to the committee, and on the criteria that the committee will employ in reviewing the reports.

A Strategic Planning Example

Let's hone in on a particular example in the planning stream of governing decisions: adopting an updated vision statement for your district, which is without question one of the preeminent governing decisions that a school board can make. Vision is commonly defined as a richly detailed picture of the school district that you aspire to create over the long run, in terms of impact on students and the community, of your district's role in the community, and of your district's administrative capacity and internal culture. Planning professionals universally agree that visioning is one of the most powerful processes that an organization can employ

in leading large-scale innovation and change; adoption of a vision statement stands at the pinnacle of organizational decision making, coming
as close as possible to "pure" governing work.

Your school board's formal decision to adopt an updated vision
statement by resolution in one of your monthly board meetings would
be the mere tip of the iceberg—the culmination of a multistep planning process involving the board, superintendent, and senior administrators. Determining exactly what steps will be taken on the
way to your district's updated vision statement and how your board
will be involved at particular points in the process should be the
result of active board–superintendent–senior administrator collaboration. The specifics of the process will depend on the desired
outcomes.

For example, the board planning committee and superintendent of a
medium-sized suburban district I worked with a couple of years ago decided that updating the district's vision for the future should be treated
as a critical milestone in the district's history. They agreed that the vision
statement should be detailed enough to serve as a driver of strategic
planning, instead of being another one of those two- or three-sentence
"pithy paragraphs" that are basically slogans. They also decided that the
visioning process should be characterized by (1) substantive board involvement in shaping the vision, primarily as a means of ensuring strong
board ownership of the ultimate product; (2) a stronger partnership with
key stakeholders in the community, such as the mayor and the chamber
of commerce CEO; and (3) wider community understanding and support for the district. With these desired outcomes as what might be
called "design drivers," this district's visioning process included the following key elements:

- The preliminary version of the district's vision was created in a
  brainstorming session at a one-and-a-half-day board–superintendent–
  senior administrator retreat, which also included the identification of strategic issues facing the district and the exploration of
  possible "strategic change initiatives" to deal with the issues.
- The superintendent and her top administrators refined and polished the statement in a half-day work session, after which it was
  touched up by the board's planning committee.

- This polished version was then sent to key stakeholders for their comments, after which the planning committee finalized the vision statement and sent it to the board for adoption.
- In subsequent months, the vision statement was "taken on the road" as a community education tool. The superintendent, board president, and members of the planning committee made a number of presentations in important community forums such as service club luncheons, focusing on the vision and its implications for the district and wider community. These community education sessions not only fostered wider understanding of the district's aspirations but also led to active dialogue on current educational issues.

Two More Examples

Two more real-life examples of school boards working in close partnership with their superintendents and senior administrators will bring home the tremendous potential of a collaborative approach to designing the governing work of the board: the board's role in the annual operational planning and budget preparation process and in financial performance monitoring. School boards all over the country have found their participation in preparation of their district's annual operating plan and budget an extremely frustrating experience, leading to the kind of dissatisfaction and irritation that can seriously erode the board–superintendent–senior administrator partnership. This need not be the case, as the example of a small rural district in the South demonstrates.

The gap between theory and practice has probably never been wider than in the operational planning and budgeting realm. On the theoretical side of the spectrum, is there any reader who has not heard the annual operating plan and budget described as the school board's "preeminent policy statement"? It obviously sets forth the district game plan for the coming year, allocating the district's dollars to specific educational and administrative functions. On the other hand, all too often school board members are confronted with a finished tome—only a few weeks before the budget must be adopted—that is so dense it defies easy understanding. The result is that many school boards, in my experience, end up merely thumbing through page after page of numbers, asking relatively minor questions about one detail or another that they have played virtually no role in creating. This is about as far away from high-impact governing as it is possible to get.

The superintendent of the rural district whose experience I am drawing on recognized that her board members were fed up with their passive and reactive role in the budget development process and that a creative solution had to be found. As a first step, the board president agreed to appoint an operational planning and budget development task force that was explicitly charged to come up with a more meaningful role for the school board in the process. Headed by a long-tenured board member with an oft-expressed interest in budgeting, this ad hoc body consisted of two other board members (one brand new, the other a more seasoned veteran), the superintendent, the district's chief financial officer (an associate superintendent), the middle school principal, and the director of curriculum and instruction.

At its organizational meeting, the budget task force familiarized itself with the current operating plan and budget document and the preparation procedures that had been followed in developing it; agreed to two key design principles it would follow in carrying out its work; and fashioned a 3-month schedule of meetings. The carefully formulated design principles were key to the success of the task force's efforts:

- First, the task force recognized that—theory notwithstanding—preparing the annual operating plan and budget was necessarily largely an administrative process with only limited opportunity for board input, basically because the operating plan and budget was 97 to 98% fixed. Going very far on the board participation front in this area would clearly impinge on administrative prerogatives, and the task force adamantly rejected any hint of a "zero-based" approach to budgeting (this approach, which essentially involves starting from point zero every year in preparing the budget, throwing the whole thing open for examination, is to my knowledge practiced successfully nowhere in the solar system).
- Second, the task force agreed that its approach should be conservative—without a hint of grandiosity, meaning that its recommendations would be very practical; they would carry a modest price tag; implementing them would be a relatively straightforward process, technically speaking, requiring no elaborate or expensive

technological investment; and implementation would be designed to cause no significant administrative disruption.

The task force's work yielded powerful results for this rural district in terms of meaningful board participation in the annual operational planning and budget preparation process—at a modest cost in time and money and without getting embroiled in disruptive change. Three of its six recommendations proved to be most useful in moving this school board in the direction of higher-impact governing:

- That the board establish a standing planning and resource development committee, with responsibility for working closely with the superintendent in designing and orchestrating board participation in all district planning—from updating the district vision at the strategic end of the planning continuum to developing and adopting the annual budget. This new committee replaced the old-time, narrowly focused finance committee, which had essentially just thumbed through recommended budgets in the past.
- That this planning and resource development committee annually host what the task force called a prebudget planning work session of the full board, meeting as a committee of the whole, along with the superintendent and her senior administrators, early in the planning process before any detailed budget figures had been developed. This half-day work session, now in its 5th year, involves the following:
  - The superintendent opens with an overview of the issues and challenges facing the district, with special attention to the financial dimension.
  - The chief financial officer reviews key expenditure and revenue assumptions driving the upcoming year's budget (such as the inflation factor being used to estimate various fixed costs). Active board discussion of these factors is encouraged.
  - Each of the senior administrators presents in his or her functional area (1) an analysis of performance during the past year; (2) operational issues deserving special board attention (e.g., in buildings and grounds, serious maintenance problems that have developed and demand action next year; in curriculum and instruction, an in-

flux of non-English-speaking students, calling for enhancements in the English as a second language program); (3) major operational innovations planned during the coming year (e.g., beefing up the English as a second language program); and (4) any significant expenditure increases being considered for the next year.

- That the new planning and resource development committee present the recommended budget document to the full board, opening with a description of the major educational and administrative goals driving the budget—paying special attention to student performance—and employing an easy-to-understand executive summary of budgeted revenues and expenditures, highlighting significant changes from the current year's operating plan and budget, and also using PowerPoint slides to enhance communication of the key points. By the way, the traditional budget tome with its myriad line-item details is still provided to board members for their examination if they are interested, but it is not the focus of the presentation.

My third case example, drawing on the experience of a major urban district, is less dramatic than the prior two, but it deals with one of the most important fiduciary responsibilities of every school board: monitoring district financial performance. Fortunately, in a board reorganization the previous year, this district had created a new board standing committee for performance oversight, with responsibility for monitoring all district performance: educational, financial, and administrative. The committee's charge from the school board, by the way, clearly mandated it to work with the superintendent in designing the processes it would employ in carrying out its monitoring function, rather than just plowing through documentation looking for problems.

This committee turned to financial reporting as its initial foray into the detailed design of board governing work. Over a period of 9 months, committee members reached agreement with the superintendent and chief financial officer on a new summary financial report that the committee would use in reporting financial performance to the full board at its monthly meetings. Organized in categories of major expenditure (e.g., instruction, building and grounds, athletics) and revenue (e.g., state subsidy, local property tax revenue), this report presented the information in an attractive and easy-to-understand format of bar charts showing budgeted versus actual figures, both year to date and monthly. In addition to numbers and percentages, the upgraded executive-level report also included a narrative section that pinpointed actual and potential issues related to district finances (e.g., an expenditure rate for building maintenance that would exhaust the allocation in that area halfway through the year) and, where appropriate, recommended corrective action.

To ensure that the performance oversight committee fully carried out its monitoring mission (and awesome fiduciary responsibility), committee members also reached agreement with the superintendent and chief financial officer on the criteria that would routinely be applied in reviewing financial reports. A clear presentation policy was adopted that would demonstrate committee accountability: the superintendent and chief financial officer would present and discuss the report in detail with the committee, but the committee would present and explain the report at regular monthly board meetings, with the chief financial officer available, of course, to answer questions. To make sure that all committee members were fully engaged in financial oversight, presenting the financial report at board meetings was regularly rotated among committee members.

DESIGN GOLDEN RULES

High-impact school boards that I've observed over the years have tended to follow four "golden rules" in designing their governing processes:

1. Wherever feasible, school board members should be involved proactively in shaping key governing products before final approval, rather than merely reviewing finished staff work, to ensure that board members are both fully exploited as a precious asset and that they truly own the products by the time they make the final decision. The three previous case examples certainly demonstrate this golden rule at work.

2. Where highly complex and high-stakes decisions are concerned, the process should include opportunities for the board, superin-

tendent, and senior administrators to engage in intensive dialogue outside the framework of the regular monthly board meeting, with enough time to thoroughly consider all facets of the issue under consideration. In this regard, note that the board in the vision example participated with the superintendent and senior administrators in a one-and-a-half-day planning retreat at which the original version of the vision statement was brainstormed. And the two standing committees whose experiences were described—planning and resource development and performance oversight—also provided board members with a forum to work through serious design issues that could not possibly have been tackled in a regular monthly board meeting.

3. The governing processes should regularly be reviewed and updated as appropriate to reflect advances in the field of governance and related fields, such as strategic planning and budgeting, and to provide newcomers to the board with an opportunity to influence the processes they will be participating in. Standing committees are an ideal place for redesign to occur, and many high-impact boards, for example, have their planning committee annually take a look at ways to fine-tune board participation in making planning decisions.

4. Designing and developing the governing work of your school board must be a truly collaborative process, involving you, your board colleagues, the superintendent, and senior administrators in an ongoing team effort aimed at a creative division of labor between the board, on the one hand, and the superintendent and senior administrators on the other. Dividing the labor is essentially a matter of fleshing out practical processes for involving the board creatively and proactively in making governing judgments and decisions without impinging on the proper role of your district's administrative staff.

FLESHING OUT YOUR ROI

Earlier in this chapter, I suggested that you, as an unpaid (most likely) volunteer dedicating considerable time and energy to the governing work of your school board, have every right to think about your return on investment (ROI) in terms of nonmonetary compensation for all the hours you devote to governing. At the head of the list, of course, is the satisfaction that comes from playing a meaningful role in doing really high-impact governing work that makes a significant difference in the affairs of your district. Accordingly, most of this first chapter addresses the collaborative design process for developing a high-impact governing role for your board.

Long experience has taught me that you can build into the design of your board's governing work certain features that will enrich your board members' ROI and in the process deepen board member satisfaction and commitment. Many boards around the country have successfully implemented governing processes that

- enable board members to grow in leadership knowledge and skills through their governing work
- ensure that board members experience significant ego satisfaction
- make sure that governing work includes a large dollop of fun along with a minimum of needless suffering

Growth

You have a right to expect to grow in terms of your leadership capacity through your service on your school board, and at the very least you should expect to acquire knowledge and skills that will make you a more effective participant on other boards in your community, or perhaps at the state and national levels as well. Although participating in well-designed governing processes will ensure that you learn a lot, many board members I have worked with pay closer attention to their own growth process. A good place to start is for you to inventory your own leadership skills and knowledge, identify areas that you need to strengthen, and attempt to steer your board work in directions that will accomplish the learning goals you've set for yourself.

I recently worked with a school board member who had identified before her election to the board that learning how to participate effectively in leading strategic change in an always changing, challenging world would serve her career goals as well as make her a more powerful contributor to whatever board she served on. So when she joined the school board she (1) became a strong advocate for upgrading the board's role in leading strategic change; (2) engineered her appointment to the ad hoc strategic planning task force, formed by the board president to work with the superintendent and the associate superintendent to enhance the district's strategic planning process, with the intention of making it a more powerful tool for leading large-scale innovation; and (3) eventually— by asking the board president—was appointed to the board's new standing planning committee, which was charged with overseeing implementation of the enhanced planning process. At this point in the game, this thoughtful, ambitious board member really is an expert in change-focused planning, and she can apply this expertise in her own business and in her service not only on the school board but also on future boards she will join.

Another school board member I know was keenly aware that he was a less than scintillating public speaker and that becoming more effective at the lectern would be a critical contribution to his career development, as well as enhance his influence on the school board and in the wider community. He made sure he was appointed to the board's standing committee on external and community relations and was instrumental in designing the board speakers bureau that resulted in regular bookings for board members to speak in pertinent community forums, such as the Lions and Rotary clubs. He was also a strong advocate for the development of a set of district PowerPoint slide presentations to help board members communicate more effectively and to make engagements less stressful for the less-experienced speakers on the board. Finally, this board member convinced the superintendent to provide an opportunity for board members to rehearse their presentations before assembled administrators, who could provide critical—albeit kind and gentle—feedback.

Ego Satisfaction

The average board member I have met over the years has significant ego needs, which is not at all unusual for the kind of high-achieving, ambitious people who serve on boards of all kinds. Altruism, although the primary force behind effective governance, will take you only so far, and if your ego needs are not met you will find yourself feeling emotionally less resilient over time, even though you might not recognize the cause. It is absolutely fair of you to expect that your superintendent and senior administrators will look for every opportunity within reason to provide you with ego-affirming experiences as a school board member, and you should not feel at all guilty about the expectation. It's just another form of nonmonetary compensation that can be provided simply and inexpensively. At a minimum, you can expect to be publicly recognized in your role as a top leader of your district: front and center at the ribbon cutting ceremony at the new middle school; quoted in the newspaper series on the contribution of education to your community's economic development efforts; interviewed on a morning talk show.

Public speaking can be an immensely ego-satisfying experience for board members, provided they are adequately supported in their work on the hustings, as I discussed earlier. And your superintendent's efforts to involve you and other school board members in meetings with key stakeholders, such as the mayor or chair of the local community college system, represent another healthy way to nurture board members' egos. Of course, board-savvy superintendents well know that if they don't provide such ego-reinforcing experiences, at least some of their board members will seek satisfaction in dysfunctional ways, such as challenging the superintendent in a public board meeting.

Having Fun and Avoiding Needless Pain

When you sign on to participate in governing your school district, you take on an awesome, high-stakes challenge, but there's no valid reason why you should not expect the governing experience to be enjoyable and relatively pain free—at least a good deal of the time. Your superintendent can help by making sure you are kept abreast of exciting developments nationally and at the state level in K–12 education, principally through the superintendent's report at the regular monthly meeting but also via e-mail briefings and occasional one-on-one lunch meetings. It is easy to get so bogged down in the trench of routine governing work that you lose sight of exciting developments in the ever-changing education "business." A more serious commitment to enriching the governing experience would be for your board to budget for member attendance at statewide and national conferences held by the National School Boards Association and its affiliated state associations.

Enriching your interpersonal experience is another way of bringing more enjoyment to your governing work. As you well know, formal board meetings are not an effective vehicle for getting to know your board and administrative colleagues at a more intimate level, and so it makes sense to build occasions for social interaction into your schedule, such as an informal reception or light meal before the regular board meeting, an annual retreat held off-site, an annual picnic, or an annual holiday party. You should also keep in mind that standing committees provide an opportunity for more informal interaction among board members and administrators than the regular monthly board meeting can allow.

Finally, with your superintendent's support, you can always add spice to regular board meetings (e.g., by featuring an exemplary program at every meeting), and you can also take steps to make the documentation flowing to your board more attractive and easier to use. For example, many boards I have worked with have reached agreement with their superintendents on the format of an executive summary that accompanies every major policy recommendation to the board. Going even further down this path, some school boards, typically through their standing committee responsible for financial and educational performance monitoring, have successfully experimented with the design of more user-friendly financial and educational performance reports.

EXPECT RESISTANCE

Although I don't want to conclude this discussion on a negative note, I do feel obliged to warn you that not all of your colleagues on the board will enthusiastically embrace the opportunity to play an active role in designing the processes they will employ in doing their governing work. In my experience, the majority will, and most members of the negative minority will eventually buy into the design process, but you are well advised to expect some resistance. For one thing, the average school board member is a very busy person, and the invitation to participate in designing the board's work in the interest of higher-impact governing will to some members raise the specter of lots of additional time and energy.

An occasional colleague of yours on the board, sad to say, will not be interested in high-impact governing, and hence not in the design process either, because he takes a narrow, old-fashioned view of governing as basically sitting back and judging the work of the superintendent and administrative staff, particularly "watching the critters so they don't steal the store." Fortunately, I have encountered very few of these essentially adversarial and negative board members, but you might run into an occasional one. More common is the board member who sincerely believes in high-impact governing but resists changes in process because—typically unconsciously—she feels threatened by the loss of influence. For example, I have run into several board members over the years who will fight to the death against replacing a poorly designed board committee (see chapter 2) with one that will strengthen the board's governing performance, very simply because the outmoded committee has been their vehicle for wielding influence on the board. This resistance can be insidious because the resister is not consciously aware of the source of the resistance and is often quite capable of coming up with plausible objections to change. One of the most common is the old saying, "If it ain't broke, don't fix it."

DEALING WITH RESISTANCE

It would not be reasonable to expect that every one of your current and future school board colleagues will support taking a thorough, systematic approach to developing the board's governing work. However, if you are seriously committed to your board's doing really high-impact governing work, your only choice is to work hard to prevent such resistance from carrying the day. Over the years, I have seen a number of simple, low-keyed strategies work well in countering antidevelopment attitudes:

- In the first place, do not be cowed into silence, no matter how strident the objections of one or more of your board colleagues to developing your board's governing work. The stakes are too high to suffer such wrongheadedness silently—not only in terms of the board's effectiveness and your satisfaction in making a difference, but more importantly in terms of educational outcomes and student performance. Experience has taught me that if you are willing to speak up on behalf of higher-impact governing, you will encourage like-minded colleagues to hop on the board development bandwagon with you. At the very least, you are likely to spark the interest of colleagues who have paid little attention to the subject of board development.

- Make a personal effort to educate your colleagues on the key elements of high-impact governing, beginning (if necessary) with the board president, who is obviously one of the most important potential champions of board development. Without appearing to be riding a hobbyhorse, you can easily bring high-impact governing work into discussions with your colleagues and share article reprints from the *American School Board Journal* and other periodicals; perhaps even share a copy of this and other pertinent books on the subject. By the way, since your superintendent's support will be a critical factor in successfully developing the board's leadership, if your superintendent appears not to be on top of recent developments in the board leadership arena, include him or her in your target audience. It is far from unusual to find a superintendent who has climbed steadily through the K–12 ranks to the top without having become much of an expert on governing.

- You can also encourage your colleagues to invest in educational programs on governance such as those offered by state and national associations. Ideally, your board will see its way clear to budgeting a modest amount to support board member education in the board's preeminent business: governing. If you are able to kindle enough interest among your colleagues on the board, it might be possible to take a larger step on the educational front: retaining the services of a board development specialist to present a half- or full-day workshop for your own board. If your budget will not support holding your own workshop, you might consider teaming up with other school boards in your region to jointly fund a larger event.

②

HABIT 2:
DEVELOP THE CAPACITY TO GOVERN

FOUR STRATEGIES

When your school board has taken the trouble to clarify its governing role and has mapped out in detail the processes for engaging board members in a meaningful fashion when making governing judgments and decisions, you have traveled a good distance on the board development road. However, your journey is far from over. High-impact school boards all over the country have taken the natural next step: investing in building the capacity of their boards to carry out the governing role they have mapped out. In this regard, they have pursued four major capacity building strategies:

1. Developing the school board as a human resource, which involves both strengthening the board's composition and building the board members' governing knowledge and skills
2. Employing well-designed board committees (actual or, in the case of really small boards, virtual) as "governing engines," doing the detailed governing work that could not possibly be accomplished in the monthly board meeting
3. Building the board's performance management capacity, fashioning detailed collective and individual governing performance standards and targets and systematically monitoring governing performance

4. Fostering stronger collaboration among board members, turning them into a more cohesive governing team

ESSENTIALLY A PEOPLE BUSINESS

Far from being an abstract entity, your school board is above all else the people serving on it, and you and your board colleagues are without question the key ingredients in the high-impact governing recipe. The commitment, energy, intelligence, knowledge, and skills that you and your colleagues bring to the boardroom make your board an enormously precious asset. Of course, a well-designed governing "machine"—your board's structure and governing processes—makes it possible to capitalize on that asset and generate the high-impact governing decisions these challenging times demand of every school district. But no matter how well designed the mechanics of your governing board are, the cast of characters making up the governing drama will always be a preeminent influence on the quality of your board's decisions. Therefore, it stands to reason that paying close attention to the composition of your board and the governing knowledge and skills of board members is one of the wisest investments you can make in promoting the cause of high-impact governing.

As you probably know, the vast majority of nonprofit boards are self-appointing, which makes board human resource development a relatively straightforward process. By contrast, the overwhelming majority of school boards are elected by the voters in their districts, making the process of influencing board composition much less direct and politically more complex. Indeed, the whole subject might at first seem off the wall to you. When I begin to discuss developing a school board's composition in workshops and speaking engagements to K–12 groups, several hands inevitably pop up, and I am advised to "stop right there! My board is elected, and there's nothing practical that my board colleagues and I can do to shape the membership of the board—at least nothing politically feasible. Give me a break: my hands are tied!"

My advice is not to throw in the towel so quickly. Not only do you have an obligation to do whatever you can to strengthen your school board as a human resource, but you can also be assured that many school boards around the country have strengthened their board's composition by taking three key steps:

1. Treating board human resource development as a formal program for which a standing school board committee is accountable
2. As part of the board's human resource development program, fashioning and keeping updated a detailed profile of the desired board composition in terms of the attributes and qualifications of individual board members
3. Employing this profile more or less directly in systematically influencing the filling of board vacancies

MORE THAN JUST THE BODIES

Before we take a look at each of these three steps, I want to point out a couple of important benefits that your school board is likely to realize from taking its development as a human resource seriously, beyond the obvious one of helping to ensure that your board consists of the people you need to do high-impact governing work. One benefit that I have seen frequently over the years is heightened board self-esteem, which tends to deepen board members' commitment to their governing work. As far as I can tell, making board human resource development a formal program with an accountable committee, and taking the trouble to fashion and use a detailed profile of the ideal board in terms of its members, tends to elevate the work of governing in the eyes of board members themselves, in a sense solemnizing their governing work.

Knowing that your school board cares enough to find the most qualified candidates to fill board vacancies makes being on the board more of an honor and a source of pride. We might not want to admit it, but ego satisfaction is an important ally of altruism in building feelings of commitment among the ambitious, high-achieving people who serve on school boards.

When your school board takes its own development as a human resource in hand, it also signals to the voters and other residents in your district, including critical stakeholder organizations such as the mayor's office and chamber of commerce, that yours is no run-of-the-mill school board. Rather, your board's meticulous attention to its own human re-source development distinguishes it from the crowd, signaling that it is an extraordinary governing body well worth serving on and working with. Such recognition can turn your school board into more of a mag-net that attracts qualified candidates as well as strengthen your board's credibility in the eyes of the public at large.

A RESPONSIBLE COMMITTEE

Many public and nonprofit boards, including public school boards, have successfully employed standing committees as governing engines that enable board members to participate in governing at a more detailed level than regular board meetings would allow. I will examine commit-tees in greater detail later in this chapter, but for now keep in mind that many boards are making good use of an executive (sometimes called gov-ernance or board operations) committee. Typically chaired by the board president and consisting of the other committee chairs and the superin-tendent, the executive committee is often charged with the responsibil-ity for board human resource development, in the following capacity:

- Ensuring that the board consists of the right mix of members who are well qualified to contribute to the governing process
- Fashioning and executing a comprehensive strategy for board member education and training
- Setting collective and individual board member performance stan-dards and monitoring performance

INFLUENCING BOARD COMPOSITION

Annually updating and formally adopting a profile of the ideal school board member is one of your strongest tools for building your school board's capacity to do high-impact governing work. Many boards I have observed over the years developed the initial profile as part of a brain-storming exercise in a retreat setting, after which the executive commit-tee refined the list and recommended it to the full board for approval. The profile basically identifies the attributes and qualifications that your board considers pertinent to the work of governing your district. Of course, you cannot expect any one person to embody all the desired traits, but it makes good sense to search for candidates that come close to the profile.

The executive committee of a school district I worked with a couple of years ago developed a profile that included such attributes and qualifications as "strongly committed to public education and to the mission of our district," "knowledgeable about current educational issues in our district," "successful experience in serving on other public and nonprofit boards," "a team player," "open-minded," "respected in the community," "demonstrated professional and/or business success," "high ethical standards," and "ties to the corporate and/or foundation community."

The point of developing a profile of the ideal school board in your district is obviously to influence the election of board members who embody the profile, in the interest of your board's doing higher-impact governing work. Without question, it would be politically untenable for a school board to become actively involved in searching for candidates fitting the profile. However, in terms of encouraging the electorate to think more seriously about the qualities of effective board members and even of attracting candidates who might otherwise not have been interested, less direct approaches have proved effective:

- Circulating the profile widely among community groups and institutions, such as civic associations, service clubs, and PTAs
- Featuring the profile in presentations to various community forums and in media appearances
- Making the profile available to a community group that is actively engaged in recruiting qualified candidates to stand for election to the school board (I lived in a school district where such a body was very effective at attracting qualified candidates)

DEVELOPING BOARD MEMBERS

The better educated and trained your school board members are in the work of governing, the more likely they are to perform at a high level. So every board that is committed to high-impact governing must also be committed to its own continuing education, dealing with two basic educational challenges:

- First, how can we make sure that new members joining our board are well prepared to hit the ground running rather than spend their 1st year on the governing job learning the ropes?
- Second, how do we keep board members' governing knowledge and skills up to date so they are able to participate productively and creatively in ongoing board capacity building?

The good news is that you could not ask for a better group of students than the people who populate your average school board. The great majority of board members I have observed over the years have been avid lifelong learners who are sincerely committed to doing a top-notch job of governing. This shouldn't come as any surprise, when you reflect on the kind of bright, high-achieving people who tend to make it to the boardroom. They are used to setting high standards and asking a lot of themselves, and they have already dedicated significant time and energy to acquiring the knowledge and skills that have contributed to their professional or business success. Slackers they are definitely not.

The bad news is that many if not most board members, in my experience, are at least initially reluctant to invest in developing their own governing knowledge and skills once they have gone through the basic orientation for new board members. This is really ironic when you think about the critical leadership role that we expect boards to play and their tremendous impact on school district performance. That the very people who would not blink an eye at investing handsomely in administrator and faculty education are capable of questioning whether they should devote time and money to their own governing education is amazing but all too often true. As far as I can tell, this is part misplaced altruism ("What happens in the classroom has first claim on our limited dollars") and part ego ("At this point, having climbed so far up the professional ladder, I really can't see myself going back to school"). Whatever the cause, truly high-impact school boards overcome the reluctance, recognizing that underinvesting in developing their governing knowledge and skills is a classic penny-wise, pound-foolish course of action.

School boards that I have seen deal effectively with this twin educational challenge have established a formal board education process, spearheaded by the board's executive committee, that consists of two elements: (1) a thorough orientation program for incoming board members and (2) a continuing education program aimed at keeping board member knowledge and skills current. I briefly discussed the concept of an executive, or governance, committee earlier in this chapter. Experience has taught me that if you want board members to pay close attention to a leadership function and really take it seriously, you will want to assign it to a board standing committee; otherwise you're unlikely to generate enough ownership and commitment to make it fly. This is what many school boards have done with the board education function, which is typically made a responsibility of the executive—or what I prefer to call governance—committee, in keeping with its overall role as the committee on board operations.

New Member Orientation

One of the questions I always ask when interviewing board members is "What does the board do to make sure that incoming members hit the ground running?" You might be surprised to learn that the answer is often "Nothing in particular." But even when the answer is "We provide new board members with an orientation," a little digging more often than not reveals that the orientation has little to do with the work of governing, which is obviously what board members spend the great majority of their time doing (or should, anyway). Instead, new board members are often briefed in detail on the programs, services, budget, administrative structure, and other facets of the organizational life of the school district, with nary a word about the board itself.

Although you obviously want incoming board members to understand the educational mission and key programmatic and operational features of the school district they are being asked to govern, what they need more than anything else if they are to succeed at the governing business is a thorough orientation on the board itself: its role, detailed governing processes, and structure. This is now being widely recognized, and many school districts these days make sure their orientation programs include such elements as the board's

- governing role (and the formal governing mission—discussed later in the chapter)
- performance targets (what is expected of individual board members)
- committee structure (the roles and detailed responsibilities of the standing committees)
- involvement points in such key processes as CEO evaluation, strategic planning, and budgeting

Although you will still see superintendents handling the orientation of incoming board members, a growing practice is for members of the executive, or governance, committee to actually conduct the orientation themselves as a means of visibly demonstrating that board education is a top priority, not just another job to be passed along to the superintendent. Assigning the orientation job to committee members also reinforces the board's accountability for managing its own performance as governing body.

Another growing practice is formal mentoring: pairing each incoming school board member with a seasoned member who plays a mentoring role for, say, the first 6 months of the new member's tenure. The mentor's major job is to make time available to discuss any questions the new board member has about the board and to provide coaching as appropriate.

Continuing Education

School governance is anything but a static field with hard and fast principles that are cast in bronze and immutable. Instead, every day that passes in this wild and wonderful (and relatively new) field sees yesterday's golden rules challenged, new principles proposed, and new approaches and techniques for generating higher-impact governance reported. Taking the time and effort to keep your board members abreast of developments in this exciting field can serve two important purposes. First, you can combat the fatigue, boredom, and even burnout that can work against high-impact governing—motivating, inspiring, and energizing your board members by raising their sights above the trenches where much of their governing work takes place.

Second, you can arm your board members with information they can put to practical use in their board organizational development efforts. For example, dramatic developments in the field of strategic planning (see chapter 3) provide board members with opportunities to play a proactive, creative role in leading strategic change, rather than merely thumbing through a finished tome on its way to the proverbial dusty shelf.

Highly effective board continuing education programs that I have observed over the years have included such elements as the following:

- A lending library of books and articles on governance that are regularly circulated among board members. In this regard, your first sources will be NSBA and AASA. Many school boards have joined BoardSource (formerly the National Center for Nonprofit Boards), which publishes short, easy-to-read guidebooks covering every conceivable facet of governing board operations. Busy board members are often more willing to read carefully selected articles than books, and it makes sense to have a staff member regularly review periodicals such as the *American School Board Journal* and *School Administrator* for articles that will enrich board member understanding of various aspects of their governing work. If time is available, you might even have staff précis articles so that board members can decide whether it's worth their while to read the whole thing.
- Participation in educational programs addressing governing matters. Both NSBA and AASA offer educational sessions on governance at their annual meetings, and many state school board associations provide training for school board members, which is increasingly state mandated. Some school districts retain consultants to present on-site educational programs for their board members exclusively, an approach that provides both stronger quality control and greater opportunity for in-depth participation—but at a price, of course.
- Building a half-day session on governance into the annual strategic planning retreat (see chapter 3), using this time to discuss recent advances in the field and to identify opportunities to fine-tune and strengthen governing structure and process.

Quality control is always a serious issue in the education business. It would obviously be counterproductive to send board members to a governing program that ends up being a sales pitch for one of those one-size-fits-all governing models that are always floating around. The most effective board continuing education programs, in my experience, build quality control into the planning—often by asking the superintendent to review potential educational offerings to ascertain if they are worth board members' time. Another issue is incentive to participate. Although board members are typically avid lifelong learners, they are also very busy people. Participation in educational programs will tend to increase, in my experience, if such participation is made a formal board member performance target (see the discussion of board performance management later in the chapter).

THOSE GOVERNING ENGINES

The topic of board standing committees probably does not grab your imagination or send shivers of excitement up and down your spine, but you would be well advised not to underestimate the powerful contribution that these governing engines can make to high-impact governing—or the harm that poorly designed committees can do. Although you will hear debate about whether it makes sense for a school board to have standing committees, the question is settled in my mind. I have never seen a truly high-impact board that functioned without well-designed standing committees, and so I have become a passionate committee advocate. I have also, by the way, seen poorly designed committees bedevil board members and superintendents, making it extremely difficult to govern at a high level and turning boards and superintendents into unwitting victims of bad structural design.

Let me assure you that I recognize that there are school boards so small (say, five or fewer members) that dividing them into standing committees would obviously not make much sense. My rule of thumb is that you need a minimum of seven board members for actual (rather than virtual) committees to make sense: three board members serving on each of two committees, with the board chair concentrating on leading the regular monthly meeting and the deliberations of the executive

committee. However, even if your board is too small to divide into actual committees, I strongly recommend virtual committees, which basically means that the full board convenes in a committee format outside
of the regular monthly board meeting: meeting as the planning committee one day, and the performance monitoring committee the other.
At the very least, this approach will ensure that preparation for the regular board meeting is more thorough, and it should not entail a net increase in board members' time commitment since better preparation
will decrease the time required for the regular monthly meeting.

Well-designed standing committees can strengthen your board's governing performance and the board–superintendent partnership in four
major ways:

1. Committees promote technically sound governing decisions, primarily by enabling board members to get into governing matters
   at a level of detail that the regular board meeting does not allow.
   For example, in following up on the annual strategic planning retreat, your planning committee can pay close attention to refining
   the values statement that was brainstormed at the retreat, putting
   it in final form for recommendation to the full board.
2. Committees build feelings of ownership and accountability among
   board members through their detailed involvement in addressing
   governing issues, taking pressure off the CEO to be the only
   source of action recommendations to the full board.
3. Committees can serve as a very effective vehicle for refining and
   strengthening the board's governing processes. For example, not
   long ago I sat in on the meeting of a board's governance committee, at which committee members and the superintendent reached
   agreement on the blow-by-blow process that the board would follow in evaluating the superintendent's performance, from the initial negotiation of superintendent leadership targets through the
   end-of-year assessment. Not long after that, I observed the deliberations of a board performance oversight committee, which resulted in a reformatted quarterly financial report that was much
   easier for board members to understand and to use.
4. Committees can also build a more cohesive board–administrator
   working relationship by facilitating sustained interaction of a less

formal nature not possible at regular board meetings. I have also seen committees strengthen the board–superintendent partnership by enabling the superintendent to develop strong working relationships with committee chairs.

COMMITTEE DESIGN

The primary job of a board standing committee is to prepare for the regular monthly school board meeting, ensuring that informational briefings and action recommendations are ready for full board review and decision making. Experience has taught me that if a standing committee is to play this important role in a full and timely fashion,

- it must be organized along governing—not programmatic or administrative—lines, corresponding to the flow of governing decisions and "products"
- its purview must be organization-wide, cutting across all programs, functions, and organizational units of the school district, thereby enabling the board to exercise what I call "horizontal discipline" in its governing work

Two broadly constituted committees that meet these two criteria have proved to be indispensable governing engines in my experience: planning (often called planning and development or planning and program development) and performance monitoring (often called performance oversight or management oversight). Your board's planning committee would be responsible for helping the board deal with a wide variety of planning decisions and "products"—everything from updating your school district's values and vision statement to adopting the annual operational plan and budget. Your board's performance monitoring committee would be responsible for helping the board assess on an ongoing basis how well your district is performing—educationally (especially student performance) and financially. You can easily see that these two committees satisfy the horizontal discipline criterion: planning covers all planning that your district does; performance monitoring tracks and assesses all activities going on in your district.

Many school boards have an executive committee, typically consisting of the board president, the chairs of the other committees, and the superintendent. The problem with the traditional executive committee is that it is often treated as a mini-board that basically screens all information going to the full board, thereby more often than not alienating other board members, who feel less important and out of the loop. Many boards in recent years have turned their executive committee (frequently called the governance committee these days) into a committee on board operations, rather than a mini-board, whose primary responsibility is to make sure that the board is functioning smoothly as a governing body.

The most effective standing committees I have observed over the years take very seriously their governing process design responsibility, in addition to carrying out their governing work (see chapter 1 for a detailed description of the design process). They collaborate closely with their superintendent and senior administrators in working through the division of labor between the board and administration to make governing decisions. For example, representing the full board, your planning committee can annually take a close look at the design of the strategic and operational planning process of your organization from the board's perspective, identifying practical enhancements that will strengthen the board's participation in making planning decisions. The planning committee might fine-tune the agenda of the annual strategic planning retreat to make it a more effective forum for the identification of strategic issues, or the performance monitoring committee might reach agreement with the superintendent on enhancements to the program performance reports that will promote stronger board understanding of district educational and financial performance.

Avoid the Silos

Violating the key design principle that standing committees should correspond to the board's governing work, rather than to the programmatic and administrative work of your school district, is a surefire way to reduce your board's governing performance. Two types of dysfunctional committees stand out as enemies of high-impact governing: (1) "tip of the administrative iceberg" committees that correspond to narrow administrative functions—for example, finance, audit, personnel, buildings and grounds; and (2) "program silo" committees that correspond to major programs or services that your district provides—for example, instruction, pupil services, athletics.

Instead of enabling your board to exercise horizontal discipline in carrying out its governing work, these poorly designed committees narrow your board members' perspectives, chopping their governing work into little pieces that don't add up—not unlike the proverbial blind person who sees an elephant as only an ear, a trunk, a tail, or a foot, missing the whole elephant completely. This poorly designed structure will inevitably turn your board into a collection of technical advisory committees, in the process actually inviting board meddling in administrative and programmatic detail.

When I encounter a defensive superintendent and administrators who are wasting precious time defending executive and administrative turf from board interference, more often than not the culprit is a poorly designed committee structure that invites board meddling. I have now and then mused about the reasons why such dysfunctional committees were ever put in place to begin with. The only explanation I have come up with is that boards were traditionally treated as an afterthought in developing organizational structure. Without seriously thinking through how committees should contribute to governing, boards were allowed to become mere vertical extensions of already developed district structure of programs and administrative functions.

Avoid the Wrong Cure

Consultants who traipse around the country advising boards and superintendents to avoid standing committees are reacting to the shortcomings of a poorly designed committee structure that promotes meddling or forces board members to spend time figuring out how to keep busy enough to justify particular committees (always the case with a committee such as personnel). The only sensible cure, in my professional opinion, for a poorly designed committee structure is a well-designed one that really does facilitate high-impact governing. Taking the extreme course of having your board function as a committee of the whole would mean losing the powerful technical and political benefits that well-designed governing engines can produce.

SOME TRIED AND TRUE GUIDELINES

The following guidelines—thoroughly tested in practice—have helped standing committees function at a high level in supporting and facilitating high-impact governing in school districts and other public and nonprofit organizations:

- Every board member should serve on one and only one standing committee—with the exception that during your term as a committee chair you will also serve on the executive, or governance, committee. If any board members are allowed to avoid committee service, it will create a caste system (those who must participate and those who are too important to have to), and where smaller boards are concerned, one or more committees might drop below a "critical mass" of members.
- The standing committees must be the only path to the full board agenda. This is a massive calcium injection, ensuring that committee work is taken seriously and that committees don't degenerate into mere discussion groups.
- All reports at full board meetings must be made by committee chairs and other committee members, with the sole exception of the superintendent's regular report. This simple requirement not only fosters committee members' ownership of reports and recommendations to the board but also ensures that committee members do their homework (not wanting, of course, to be embarrassed in public). There is the added benefit of the ego satisfaction that comes from committee members' visible leadership at board meetings.
- The superintendent should assign a senior administrator to serve as chief staff member to each committee, ensuring that the committee is provided with the staff support required to carry out its governing work in a full and timely fashion.

TAKING FORMAL ACCOUNTABILITY

Performance accountability is a hallmark of high-achieving organizations and individuals; they set high standards, monitor their own performance, and take concrete steps to become better at what they do. School boards are no exception. Every truly high-impact board I have ever worked with has played an active, formal role in managing its own performance as a governing body, not only taking accountability for the board's collective performance but also making sure that individual board members meet well-defined performance targets. Although the superintendent must be actively involved in supporting the development of school board governing capacity, no superintendent in his or her right mind would attempt to set board performance standards or hold board members accountable for meeting them. This is a job that your school board must handle for itself.

Rigorous board self-management is not only a surefire way to enhance governing performance, it can also build a more positive internal board culture and a positive public image. For one thing, the members of boards that take accountability for their own performance tend to become stronger owners of their governing work, and hence grow more firmly committed to their governing mission. The internal culture of such accountable boards, in my experience, is also characterized by higher self-esteem and esprit de corps, for the simple reason that the high-achieving people who populate boards are emotionally attracted to setting and meeting standards. After all, that is one of the key reasons for their professional and business success—and for their making it to the board in the first place.

You do not want to underestimate the impact that an accountability culture can have on your school board's human resource development. I am often asked the following question in my governance workshops: "Won't some of the really outstanding people we'd like to get on our board be turned off by the whole idea of having their performance measured? After all, these are pretty important people, and we don't want to alienate them." My answer is always the same: "Don't worry; holding your board to clear, precise performance standards will have the opposite effect. The more illustrious the candidate for board membership, the more attractive performance management will be for him or her."

Boards that formally and systematically hold themselves to account for their governing performance tend to become magnets that attract the attention of qualified candidates. In my experience, the word inevitably gets around pretty widely in your community that your board is a cut above the ordinary governing body. Potential board members who highly value their time, and hence are looking for a really productive and satisfying governing experience, will tend to be especially interested in standing for election to your board because of its reputation for rigorous self-management.

No matter how committed the individuals on your board are to performance accountability, however, formality and structure are critical. Individual board members cannot realistically be expected to hold each other to account, as you well know; life is just too short to take on the task of trying to critique and correct erring colleagues. In the absence of a formally established and managed accountability program, as you have no doubt learned over the years, board members will tend to sit back and tolerate unsatisfactory performance rather than risk alienating colleagues. Your school board's accountability program need not be elaborate, consisting very simply of the following:

- A responsible committee
- Formally developed and adopted performance targets and standards for the board collectively and for individual board members
- Systematic monitoring
- Continuous improvement

The Responsible Committee

Assigning responsibility for board performance management to a standing committee takes the matter out of the realm of interpersonal politics, making the process of setting standards and monitoring performance politically workable. The boards of many school districts and other public and nonprofit organizations have assigned this responsibility to the board's executive, or governance, committee, in keeping with its role as the committee on board operations. Headed by your board president and consisting of the standing committee chairs, perhaps other board officers, and the superintendent, the executive committee brings both clout and credibility to the performance management task. You just want to make sure that the accountability management role is clearly spelled out in the official committee position description, which should be formally adopted by the whole board.

Dealing with Collective Performance Targets

With regard to your board's collective performance as a governing body, many boards that have done an effective job of managing their own governing performance have started with what I call the "governing mission," which is a detailed statement of the desired outcomes and impacts of your board's governing work, completing the sentence, "As a result of our efforts as a board . . ." Board governing mission statements have, for example, included such elements as "a clear, detailed values and vision statement," "a portfolio of strategic change initiatives that is updated annually," "annual evaluation of superintendent performance," and "rigorous monitoring of educational and financial performance." An intensive board–superintendent–senior administrator retreat is an ideal venue for developing a rough cut of your board's first governing mission, after which the governance committee can refine it and recommend its adoption by the full board. Thereafter, it makes sense for the executive, or governance, committee to update the statement every few years, recommending readoption by the board.

What the governing mission provides is a high-level checklist of your board's responsibilities. With the mission in hand, your executive, or governance, committee can go down the list of items, asking: (1) are we addressing each of the mission elements as a board? and (2) how well are we addressing each one? Many boards have gone beyond the checklist approach (I strongly recommend doing so) by asking their standing committees to develop more precise board performance targets for the mission elements within their purview and to bring the targets to the executive, or governance, committee for review and concurrence.

For example, your board's planning and development committee would reach agreement with your superintendent on the strategic and operational planning process and calendar, which, among other things, would define what is meant by a values and vision statement and specify how it is to be updated. Your board's performance oversight committee would naturally be responsible for determining how the annual external audit process will be handled (essentially, how a firm will be selected and how the report will be reviewed and corrective actions handled). And your board's executive, or governance, committee would be the natural place to handle the superintendent evaluation process.

A two-tiered approach to assessing your board's collective perform-ance as a governing body has worked well in practice. First, each of the standing committees in a special work session assesses its governing performance in its respective areas, notes problematic performance, and suggests corrective steps to improve performance. For example, the planning committee of a board I worked with not long ago deter-mined that follow-up to the last annual strategic planning retreat had not been handled well in certain respects, particularly the process of re-viewing and winnowing down the list of strategic issues. The commit-tee recommended that the design of the next year's retreat include a more methodical process of brainstorming and analyzing strategic is-sues and that the planning committee utilize a task force of nonboard community volunteers to come up with a recommended short list for committee review. The executive, or governance, committee can dis-cuss the individual committee assessments, develop the final board re-port card, and bless the recommended corrective actions that the com-mittees have developed.

Dealing with Individual Performance

Many board members, in my experience, feel quite a bit of trepida-tion about the prospect of evaluating their colleagues' individual per-formance, worrying that they might offend their peers or, worse, cause someone to leave the board rather than subject himself or herself to per-formance evaluation. In practice, however, I have never seen individual board member performance assessments produce negative results. On the contrary, committed, hard-working board members welcome their performance being monitored; after all, formal performance assessment is a way of both elevating the importance of the governing role while also honoring hard work and dedication.

What I have found objectionable to those board members who make a real effort to participate productively and creatively in the governing process is a board culture that allows substandard per-formance to go unnoticed and uncorrected. Not setting individual board member performance standards and monitoring performance, in the eyes of productive board members, demeans the governing function by saying, in effect, that any level of performance is good enough and shows disrespect for those who do care enough to do their very best in the cause of good governing.

The process need not be elaborate or in any way punitive to accomplish the intended result of contributing to higher-impact governing work on your board. The first set of individual board member performance targets and standards can be developed in a retreat, refined by the executive committee, and eventually adopted by the full board. Thereafter, the executive committee can tweak the performance targets now and then. One board I worked with a few years ago included the following on its list of targets:

- Missing no more than one full board or committee meeting during any fiscal year, with the exception of a family emergency
- Always coming to meetings prepared to participate fully
- Participating in at least one of the graduation ceremonies annually
- Attending the annual two-day strategic work session kicking off the planning cycle
- Making at least three presentations per year on behalf of the district to key stakeholder organizations in the community

The objective of the monitoring process is to flag substandard performance before it becomes habitual and to provide counsel aimed at correcting it, without causing any embarrassment to erring board members. In my experience, it makes sense for the executive, or governance, committee to make individual board member performance a formal agenda item at least quarterly, taking a management by exception approach. Standing committee chairs are ideally positioned to observe board member performance, and one of their key responsibilities should be to bring instances of poor performance to the attention of the executive committee at the quarterly assessment session.

The really good news, in my experience, is that 99.99% of board members rise to the occasion. They come to the governing game willing and able to perform the governing role conscientiously, and so setting standards and targets is a self-fulfilling activity. The 0.01% that fall short are the exception that proves the rule.

BOARD TEAM BUILDING

Teamwork in the abstract is neither here nor there. The only serious reason for developing your board's teamwork is to help it function as a more effective governing body that gets its governing work done more effectively and efficiently. The acid test of an effective team is its productivity in accomplishing its assigned tasks, and productive teams are generally characterized by a high level of cooperation and coordination in getting their work done, harmonious relations among team members, the absence of debilitating conflicts, and the capacity to withstand considerable stress and strain without falling apart.

Although it makes sense for your school board to pay focused attention to becoming a more effective governing team, you would be well advised not to carry team building too far. You obviously would not want to eliminate all tension or even occasional conflict from your board's governing process. In today's changing, challenging world, which places a premium on your school board's dealing with highly complex governing issues, the last thing you want is a board of "good little boys and girls" who placidly go along with staff recommendations without asking the really tough questions.

MEETING THE CHALLENGE

Turning a diverse group of people with varied backgrounds, experience, expertise, and affiliations into a cohesive governing team can be a daunting task, especially in the world of K–12 public education, primarily because the constituency representation mindset that is so strong a part of school board culture in many communities creates a centrifugal force that works against team building. I have observed all too many school boards over the years whose members thought of themselves as more accountable to segments of the community than to their colleagues as a governing team.

In my experience, three strategies have proved most useful in building cohesive board governing teams:

1. Focusing on ultimate governing ends
2. Following teamwork guidelines
3. Developing emotional bonding

Focusing on the Ends

Experience has probably taught you, as it has me, that members of a team tend to be more committed to their team's work when they clearly understand the ultimate purposes the team is intended to serve. There is no reason to believe that school boards are any exception, and, in fact, the ones I have observed that do have a handle on their governing purposes really do function as stronger governing teams. Many school board members would say that the ultimate purposes of their governing efforts, which are often conveyed in the board mission statement described earlier in this chapter, are to ensure student achievement, district financial stability, and a high level of community support. Codifying these ultimate ends—for example, in a formal board mission statement—and keeping them front and center in board deliberations is a powerful team-building tool.

At a more pedestrian level, the immediate results of your school board's governing work, which can be stated in terms of achieving the collective governing performance targets described earlier in this chapter, can also serve as a team-building vehicle. The fact is, considerable teamwork is required for board members to play a creative and proactive role in annual operational planning and budget preparation or in updating your district's vision statement.

Teamwork Guidelines

Many districts have found that putting together a set of simple, straightforward guidelines to govern board member interactions is an effective, inexpensive tool for strengthening board teamwork. A common approach is to develop the initial set of guidelines in a retreat setting and, after they have been refined and adopted, to update them every year or so. One board's guidelines included, for example, "open, honest, frequent communication," "respect for each other's viewpoints and opinions," "no hidden agendas," "support for the majority's decisions even if you disagree," and "adherence to the formal governing structure and process established by the board."

Guidelines are not worth the paper they are written on unless your board pays attention to their observance. In this regard, many boards have assigned their executive, or governance, committee responsibility for monitoring board teamwork.

Emotional Bonding

Strangers do not make good team members, and building greater intimacy among your board members is a proven way to grease the interaction wheels and help your board get through traumatic situations largely unscathed. Building emotional ties among school board members is a real challenge because of the limited amount of direct interaction, but many districts have successfully narrowed the distance among board members by taking simple steps such as the following:

- Asking every board member to supply a detailed biographical sketch, covering both professional and personal details, and putting the sketches together in a handbook distributed to all board members
- Adding informal social interaction to regular board business meetings, for example, over lunch or dinner at which no business is discussed
- Holding an annual one- or two-day retreat away from district headquarters—with considerable breakout group work built in as a means to foster active interaction
- Employing standing committees of the board as a way to strengthen interaction through small group work involving less formality than full board meetings

3

HABIT 3: PLAY AN ACTIVE ROLE IN LEADING INNOVATION AND CHANGE

THE CHANGE IMPERATIVE

I have told my now-grown children on numerous occasions that they are fortunate to live and work in today's world, and I am downright serious. Never in human history—at least in contemporary America—have people had so much freedom and such a wide range of choices, not only in careers but socially and culturally as well. And dramatic technological advances have made capitalizing on opportunities and exercising choice easier by the day. We are, indeed, fortunate these days, especially if we are perceptive about environmental change, flexible in our responses, not fearful of change, and have enough courage to take advantage of opportunities.

However, whatever benefits it brings, change does have a darker side, of course. The magnitude and pace of demographic, economic, technological, social, and cultural change definitely complicate your role as a school board member who is responsible for setting directions that will promote your district's educational effectiveness and its financial and political stability. Leading school districts in these rapidly changing times is extremely challenging because, as board members, you are constantly bombarded with issues—"change challenges" if you will—that call for your immediate attention. Indeed, you can think of leading innovation and change as, in essence, responding to emerging and full-blown issues that come in the form of opportunities (your district is invited to join a city-led economic development coalition being formed to attract new firms to your community; you are eligible to apply for a huge state grant) and threats (a rapid increase in the number of childless households in your district or of single-parent households whose growth is accompanied by steadily dropping family income levels). No Child Left Behind would be an excellent example of an issue that represents both opportunity and threat, depending on your perspective.

These issues that penetrate your consciousness and the consciousness of your board colleagues all come with an implied question to you as a board member: Should we initiate innovation and change to address one or another issue? Or is inaction a safe course, at least for the time being? There will always be change challenges that your district cannot afford to ignore because the cost of inaction will be too high, in terms of significant educational shortfalls, out-of-pocket costs, lost revenue, tarnished reputations, and the like. Thus, you and your school board colleagues will always be facing a stark choice:

Either play a leading role—hand in hand with your superintendent and senior administrators—in leading your district's innovation and change efforts

-or-

sit on the sidelines, thereby not only missing a huge piece of the leadership action but also putting your district at risk of becoming the victim—rather than the leader—of change.

As you have probably learned by now in your school board career, there is no middle ground in today's changing, challenging, and often threatening world. If you and your board colleagues do not master the change game, systematically exercising some measure of influence over your district's destiny, you will eventually be changed anyway by the forces around your district. And experience has taught that changes forced on an organization from the outside, rather than planned and managed by the organization, are likely to be traumatic, coming at a high cost in pain and suffering.

GO FOR IT!

You and your colleagues on the school board owe it to yourselves to join your superintendent and senior administrators on your district's change leadership team, for four very compelling reasons:

1. You and your school board colleagues are uniquely qualified to play a creative and proactive role in leading your district's change. The evidence is in: Effective leadership of innovation and change tremendously benefits from the diversity of experience, expertise, knowledge, and perspectives that characterize the average school board. This is one of the most important reasons why larger, more diverse boards tend to make a stronger contribution to the change process than smaller, less diverse governing bodies. Big is always better at the top in the change business.

2. Unlike most of the work involved in operational planning and budgeting, which is by its very nature more constrained and administrative in nature, providing only limited opportunity for creative school board involvement, innovation and change leadership offers your board the opportunity to make a significant difference in the affairs of your district. Indeed, in my opinion it is the "gold standard" for school board involvement, with no close second as a vehicle for creative board involvement in doing high-impact governing work.

3. Your and your board colleagues' collective authority and prestige as the governing body of your district are needed to carry out significant change, not only because implementing change normally requires funding and your board holds the purse strings but also because your superintendent is likely to need your strong backing in dealing with inevitable internal resistance to change.

4. You and your colleagues also deserve to share in the excitement, satisfaction, and even fun that—despite the stress and strain— come with grappling with really juicy issues. In-depth board participation in leading innovation and change is one of the most important forms of nonmonetary compensation that you have earned for all your governing efforts.

THE PREREQUISITES

What do you and your board colleagues need to become effective collaborators with your superintendent and senior administrators in leading your district's innovation and change efforts? School boards that I have seen succeed as change leaders over the years have done the following:

- Clearly chosen to make participating in innovation and change leadership a high priority, explicitly committing significant time to playing a leadership role in leading district change.
- Selectively played an intensive, hands-on role in the innovation and change process. This does not mean that they have competed with their superintendent and senior administrators in doing detailed planning. Rather, working closely with the superintendent, they have identified points where proactive involvement of the school board adds real value (e.g., updating the district's vision statement and identifying issues in a retreat setting), and they have concentrated their hands-on involvement at these points, retreating to a more traditional reactive role where appropriate (e.g., review by the board's planning committee of detailed implementation strategies recommended by the superintendent).
- Taken the trouble to become knowledgeable enough about the field of innovation and change leadership that they can play a meaningful part in shaping their role in the change process. A knowledgeable school board will never get caught up in a traditional long-range planning process as a substitute for serious change leadership.
- Made effective use of a board planning committee as a vehicle for design of the board's role—and detailed involvement—in the change process (see chapter 2).

A WORD ON INNOVATION AND CHANGE

You might be wondering at this point in the discussion why I have been using the phrase "innovation and change," which might seem redundant since the two are often used synonymously. Without any desire to split hairs, I assure you that I am making an important and highly practical distinction between *innovation* and *change* that will make the best of sense as this chapter goes on. I use the word *innovation* in this chapter—and in my work with public and nonprofit organizations generally—to describe the process of coming up with new responses to address the change challenges confronting your district. In this sense, the product of the innovation process is a planned "change initiative," such as an image-building strategy to address a perceived dramatic decline in public support in your district (as evidenced by recent surveys or, more dramatically, by the failure of two tax issues on the ballot over the past 18 months) or a huge investment in computer technology to deal with abysmal student performance. The innovation process, therefore, generates change plans but does not produce change per se.

I employ the word *change* to describe the process of carrying out innovation: actually implementing the planned initiatives that have resulted from the innovation process. In my professional experience, organizations, including many school districts I have observed, that fail to make this critical distinction between innovation and change—and to put it into practice—are all too likely to end up with ambitious planning tomes that sit on the proverbial dusty shelf (who has not seen plenty of these over the years?), little consulted and certainly making no significant difference in organizational affairs. Indeed, innovating change and managing change are two very different processes, requiring different methodologies and facing different sets of barriers.

Innovation—coming up with planned change initiatives—requires aggressive intelligence gathering to identify the issues floating around in your environment; open-mindedness, so that you do not filter out issues; and creative brainstorming of a variety of responses to the issues rather than jumping to the most obvious answers or falling victim to preconceived notions. The innovation process, therefore, thrives on the use of retreats that involve participants in ample brainstorming and that avoid premature decision making. Make note: This is an ideal situation for creative board involvement. The barriers to successful innovation are narrow-mindedness, allegiance to "pet" solutions, and the discomfort and occasional keen anxiety that come from thinking "out of the box."

Type A personalities who are passionate about quickly tying every loose end tend to resist the innovation process, for obvious reasons. As a retreat facilitator, I have become accustomed to participants in brainstorming breakout groups erupting in anger now and then as their discomfort peaks (anger always being preferable to feeling threatened to the type A personality).

Change—putting planned innovation initiatives into action—requires oodles of discipline as detailed implementation plans are crafted and executed. The opportunity for proactive, intensive board participation is more limited than in the innovation process—confined largely to reviewing recommended strategies, committing the resources to their implementation, and backing the superintendent and senior administrators as they contend with the inevitable resistance that any significant change tends to elicit.

You never want to underestimate how strong resistance to change is likely to be, even among the most committed and well-meaning people. I will never forget the resistance I felt as a teacher of English as a second language in Ethiopia some 30 years ago, when the glaring failure of my traditional teaching methods (learning through reading excerpts from the classics), in terms of tested student performance, forced me to adopt a programmed learning approach involving drilling students to the nth degree. In my head I saw the change in instructional approach as imperative; in my heart, I felt out of place and terribly threatened. I have seen the keen resistance I felt at work countless times in different settings over the years since I taught at Tafari Makonnen Secondary School in Addis Ababa. I have concluded that you should always expect people to resist behaving in new ways, probably because, more than anything else, they fear failure and are especially afraid of being seen as less than competent and in command.

TWO INNOVATION AND CHANGE STREAMS

I have defined innovation as the process of coming up with new responses—change initiatives—to address emerging and full-blown issues facing your school district, and change as the process of implementing these change initiatives. Later in this chapter, I will take a close look at the planning methodologies your district can employ in producing innovation and change—with special focus on the points in the process where the participation of your school board will yield the most powerful results. For now, I want to suggest a useful way of categorizing innovation and change efforts that goes beyond the traditional "strategic" and "tactical" labels. Too often in the past, the term *strategic* has simply been used to describe the output of the traditional comprehensive long-range planning process, while the term *tactical* has been used to describe any other (presumably shorter-term and lower-impact) change. As I discuss in the following section, traditional long-range planning has tended not to generate significant innovation, so as a school board member you would certainly want to be wary of relying on it as an innovation vehicle.

Let me suggest that you think of innovation and change as flowing along two broad streams that have proved useful to leaders of all kinds of public and nonprofit organizations in recent years:

- *Operational innovation and change*
  In real life, if not in theory, the great majority of issues facing your school district over the years can be handled through your district's tried and true operational planning and budget preparation process, which can be a highly effective means of handling the bulk of your district's innovation and change efforts in any given year. As I will discuss later in this chapter, you and your board colleagues can certainly play a creative role in this process of operational innovation and change, although by its very nature the administrative role will be much larger and your role as a school board member relatively constrained. For example, in a prebudget work session that your board's planning committee hosts to kick off the operational planning and budget preparation process, you might very well find yourselves discussing innovations in the use of computer-assisted instruction or class scheduling that can be implemented to address student performance shortfalls. You can call these innovations tactical if you want, but the meaningful distinction is that the innovation and change can be handled through the normal operational planning process. And you should keep in mind that the change that takes place in the operational planning "stream," although it occurs within established organizational (a particular

building; the curriculum and instruction department) and programmatic (pupil services, athletics) boundaries, can have tremendous long-term impact even though it did not result from a so-called strategic planning process.

- *Above-the-line innovation and change*
  However, you and your school board colleagues, in close collaboration with your superintendent and senior administrators, will always encounter issues you would not want to entrust to your district's operational planning and budget preparation process. These strategic issues tend to be
  - high-stakes, in the sense that not addressing them will very likely come at a high cost to your district, in terms of out-of-pocket dollars (a lost tax levy), lost opportunity (a large grant not applied for), or reputation (loss of public support)
  - highly complex, calling for "out-of-the-box" innovation, interdisciplinary and interorganizational task forces to develop change initiatives, and rigorous management of implementation
  - bureaucratic "misfits," meaning that it would not make sense to assign them to a particular district function or department

  No Child Left Behind certainly qualifies as a strategic issue, satisfying all three of these criteria.

Your board, superintendent, and senior administrators must address two serious process design challenges to ensure that the above-the-line innovation and change stream actually produces powerful results for your district in terms of effectively addressing critical issues. First, you must make sure that you have in place a reliable process for identifying these strategic issues. This is no small challenge, since experience (and plenty of serious research by change gurus such as Rosabeth Moss Kanter at the Harvard Business School) has taught that it is all too easy to miss the really strategic issues, which can be crowded out by a very normal preoccupation with operational matters and a mental filter that blocks perceptions. Second, you and your colleagues need to ensure that you have created a reliable process for the development and implementation of change initiatives. This is where traditional long-range planning has largely failed.

BYE-BYE MONSTER PLANS

Although I view conspiracy theories with healthy skepticism, I do wonder if somewhere in a Soviet ministry, perhaps industry or agriculture, some 60 or 70 years ago during the Stalinist era, a sinister anti-American plot was hatched that makes *The Manchurian Candidate* look minor league by comparison. It was, in my fantasy, chillingly simple: infiltrate the United States with Soviet agents disguised as long-range planners, whose horrifying mission was to propagate the practice of comprehensive long-range planning for arbitrary (and meaningless) periods such as 3, 5, or even 10 years. This insidious process would be ballyhooed as "strategic planning" that would give organizations firmer control of the future—an enticing aim in a world of escalating and increasingly threatening change. I imagine a trio of Soviet bureaucrats—Ivan, Dmitri, and Irina, let's say—chortling as they envision the results: "Not only will these capitalist pigs waste millions of precious hours writing bloated planning documents that end up making no real difference, they will also deforest much of their country producing these monster plans!"

I doubt that the Soviets were ingenious enough to launch such a devastating blow in the Cold War, but the facts speak for themselves: comprehensive long-range (typically 5-year) planning is generally considered a failure in terms of generating significant innovation and actually implementing change initiatives. It is quite possible that no other management process in human history has chewed up so much time, generated so many pages, and eliminated so many trees to so little effect. No wonder that two of the preeminent for-profit practitioners of formal, comprehensive long-range planning, General Electric and IBM, along with many other illustrious corporations, no longer produce monster plans. You should never forget that IBM was practicing the traditional approach when it managed to miss the PC revolution; only its legendary brainpower and immense corporate financial resources got it back in the game.

Lest you think I am setting up a paper tiger to make a point, be advised that a number of public and nonprofit organizations, including school districts, still waste precious time producing traditional long-range plans. And there are certainly consultants traipsing around, happy to assist in producing these monster documents. So there is always a clear and present danger of being sold the proverbial bill of goods. My advice: caveat emptor. Why the persistence of an obviously ineffective approach to innovation and change? My theory is that the very normal need for security and control in a dramatically changing world makes formal planning, especially for a certain time, very appealing. Despite the challenges swirling around our organization, at least we have managed to get the next 5 years under control, and we can relax and feel less anxious about the future.

The basic reason why comprehensive long-range planning for arbitrary, meaningless periods such as 5 years has been such a weak innovation device is that it takes an organization's current programs and services—in their current organizational compartments—and projects them into the future. Not only is the future unknowable 5 years hence, meaning that such projections—with few exceptions—become mechanistic and essentially useless, but also the level of detail has always driven out the issues that do not fit within the established programmatic and administrative boundaries. Merely reading the bloated tomes that such a process generates is a masochistic exercise; their futility adds insult to injury. No wonder they sit on shelves, consulted infrequently if at all, and are usually only trotted out to demonstrate to external audiences (such as the state education department) that the organization cares enough to do serious planning—pounds of it.

I have told many audiences about a research project I worked on years ago that was my first introduction to the futility of comprehensive long-range planning. I conducted an in-depth study of the experience of a large postsecondary educational institution over 5 years in implementing its comprehensive 5-year planning process. It was a classic of the genre: each unit within each campus updating a 5-year goals statement and projecting levels of effort year by year for the next 5 years; the compilation of these unit plans into campus plans, which were further compiled into the institution's 5-year plan of advancement, handsomely bound and filled with attractive and informative graphics. The plan even opened with a very strategic-like environmental scan, identifying and assessing the implications of major conditions and trends in the community. This scan had been made available to all unit heads so that they would have a context for their planning.

My research focused on the effectiveness of this meticulously designed and capably executed planning process in generating innovation and getting change initiatives implemented. My approach was to identify every major (in terms of dollars) investment the institution had made over 5 years in doing something significantly new (a program, a service, a building) and to determine what processes were followed in coming up with the change initiatives. What I learned was that not one innovation had been generated by the institution's elaborate long-range planning process; every one was developed outside the process, which merely codified the initiatives in the formal plan. Every interview I conducted with the faculty and administrators who were involved in the innovations indicated that the formal process actually impeded innovation by claiming inordinate time for merely mechanistically projecting the conventional wisdom into the future.

Let me bring this discussion of monster plans to a close by observing that I am not suggesting that you never need detailed long-range plans in your school district, and I certainly recommend long-range trends analysis as a strategic tool for identifying critical issues. For example, if demographic trends in your community indicate enrollment growth at a certain level, your school board might very well take your superintendent's recommendation to commence with a building project, and you might very sensibly put a 5-year (or 10, 8, 7) construction project in place. Or if a 5-year projection of revenue and expenditure trends indicates a potential serious deficit (with all the painful cutbacks this implies) 4 years out, your board will certainly work closely with your superintendent to come up with initiatives to deal with this strategic issue (perhaps a combination of cost control and revenue enhancement). My point is that these examples are a far cry from comprehensive long-range planning for your whole district.

A DRAMATIC ADVANCE IN INNOVATION
AND CHANGE PLANNING

A dramatic advance in the field of strategic planning in recent years makes it possible for public and nonprofit governing boards, including your school board, to play a meaningful high-impact role in leading innovation and change in your district, going well beyond merely thumbing through a finished two-pound long-range planning tome. This variation on the broad strategic planning theme, which is especially promising in terms of creative school board involvement, is what I call the "strategic change portfolio" approach. The defining characteristic of this relatively new planning approach, which has been successfully tested in many public and nonprofit organizations, is that it results in a strategic portfolio consisting of above-the-line change initiatives developed to address particular high-priority issues that the board has played a strong role in identifying.

These strategic initiatives are essentially change projects, consisting of action strategies and budgets, that are managed separately from day-to-day operational management so they are not lost in the shuffle. Each project has a different time frame, and year-to-year projects are implemented, thereby disappearing from the portfolio, and new projects are added to address new issues. For example, your school district's strategic change portfolio might consist of four key change initiatives or projects such as the following:

1. The development and implementation of a new English as a second language program in your district, utilizing a special state grant, to respond to the dramatic growth of the Latino community in the district: a 12-month initiative
2. The implementation of major board enhancements aimed at strengthening the board's governing role, including the implementation of a new committee structure: a 6-month initiative
3. The development and implementation of a partnership with the regional economic development commission, aimed at tying K–12 education explicitly into efforts to attract new firms to the region: an 18-month initiative
4. An extensive renovation of the fourth-grade curriculum and related improvements in instructional methodology, aimed at beefing up seriously lagging student performance: a 24-month initiative

THE STRATEGIC CHANGE PORTFOLIO PROCESS

The strategic change portfolio process typically begins with a board–superintendent–senior administrator retreat that kicks off two planning streams that proceed concurrently: the above-the-line portfolio process and the normal operational planning and budget preparation process, which continue along their parallel planning tracks after the retreat. Since the kickoff retreat provides your school board with its single most important opportunity to exert creative, proactive influence in the innovation and change process, I will describe how to bring off a successful retreat in the following section. For now, what you need to know is that the retreat can generate powerful drivers of the innovation process, including the following:

- An updated vision statement for your district that can serve as a framework for identifying strategic issues facing your district, which can be thought of as opportunities to move toward achieving particular elements of your district's vision or as major problems, barriers, and threats that might seriously impede progress in putting your district's vision into practice. For a vision statement to serve as a useful planning tool, it must be much more than merely a two- or three-sentence statement intended to inspire and motivate "the troops" and the wider public. A serious vision statement consists of several elements that paint a picture of the school district you aspire to create over the long run, in terms of the ultimate outcomes your district's efforts are to produce. Examples include:
  - Student performance at every grade level that exceeds state performance standards and average national performance
  - Active, steadily growing parental involvement in our district from the time their children enter kindergarten through their twelfth-grade graduation
  - Strong community support of our school district as evidenced by a willingness of residents to tax themselves to support the district
- Review and assessment of internal and external conditions and trends that are pertinent to your district's mission.
- Identification and discussion of major issues facing your district, regarding both internal and external conditions and trends.
- Discussion of possible change initiatives.

After the retreat, your district's normal operational planning and budget preparation process moves forward, while along a completely separate but parallel track, the process of updating your district's strategic change portfolio begins. The first major follow-through step, applying to both of the planning tracks, is to analyze the several issues identified in the kickoff retreat, determining which ones it makes sense to channel to the operational planning and budget preparation process (because the judgment is made that they can be handled quite well there) and which ones merit further consideration as part of the above-the-line innovation process. Many boards rely on the superintendent and senior administrators to do the issue analysis and to recommend the disposition of issues to the boards' planning committees, which make the ultimate determination of where the issues will be sent.

The next step in the process is for the superintendent and senior administrators to analyze the selected above-the-line issues and to recommend which ones will be addressed during the current planning process by fashioning detailed change initiatives that will be managed through the district's strategic change portfolio. Since a school district's financial and other resources are both finite and scarce, selectivity is critical. The point is not to generate a shopping list of attractive strategic goals; rather, it is to eventually end up with a small number of strategic change initiatives—perhaps no more than three or four—that will be added to your district's portfolio this year. The objective is not to shoot high and miss but to actually implement every change initiative in the portfolio. Many boards rely on their planning committees to work with the superintendent and senior administrators in making this determination. In doing so, one key question is typically asked about every issue on the list as part of this analysis and selection process:

> What price is my district likely to pay if we do not tackle this issue, in terms of both direct penalties (such as failure to meet state standards and eventual loss of revenue) and indirect costs (such as losing an opportunity to generate grant income)?

Of course, most school boards and administrators will rank issues the highest that have the largest and most direct impact on their district's educational bottom line: their students' performance. And at the head of this top-priority list of issues would be any that will directly impact a district's capacity to finance its educational efforts.

Once your board's planning committee has reached agreement with the superintendent on the issues that will be tackled in the current planning cycle, intensive board involvement necessarily recedes as administrators and faculty move forward—often through ad hoc task forces—to fashion strategic change initiatives to address the selected issues. From this point on, board involvement in the portfolio process, with the planning committee taking the lead, normally entails reviewing recommended change initiatives and allocating the resources required to implement them.

MAKING THE ANNUAL PLANNING RETREAT WORK FOR YOUR BOARD

Retreats have become a popular vehicle for involving school board members, their superintendents, and senior administrators in accomplishing high-impact governing work that could not be accomplished—at least not as well—in regular board business meetings. Updating a vision statement and identifying and discussing strategic and operational issues certainly fall in this category. The return on your district's investment of time, energy, and money in a retreat can be quite powerful, in terms not only of substantive outcomes such as an updated vision statement but also of process spin-offs such as esprit de corps, satisfaction, ownership of—and commitment to—directions coming out of the retreat, and even emotional bonding among participants.

However, just because you assemble the right cast of characters in an attractive retreat setting away from headquarters for a day or two does not mean you will automatically realize a powerful return on your investment in the event. Be forewarned: Retreats are high-risk affairs that can easily fall apart, doing far more harm than good, if they are not meticulously designed and conducted. The last thing you need is one of those "retreats from hell" that leave everyone with a sense of having wasted precious time and energy for naught. I will never forget interviewing members of a client board several years ago who had suffered through a terrible retreat experience 5 years earlier. What amazed me was how long the bad taste had lasted. I heard essentially the same tale from every board member I talked with. It went something like this: "We spent a whole morning debating every word in a one-paragraph vision statement and the afternoon pasting green, yellow, and red dots on flip-chart sheets taped on the walls. If you put us through this again, you'll be run out of town on a rail!"

Over the years, experience has taught me that rigorously following five golden rules will ensure that your retreat pays off handsomely for your organization without putting it at risk:

1. Make sure your board is involved in putting together the detailed retreat design.
2. Employ a professional facilitator.
3. Use well-designed breakout groups to generate content, promote feelings of ownership, and foster active participation.
4. Avoid reaching premature formal consensus or making final decisions.
5. Agree on the follow-through process at the beginning.

Retreat Design

Many school districts have taken the approach of creating an ad hoc retreat design committee to ensure board member involvement in fashioning a detailed retreat design: the specific objectives to be achieved (e.g., identification of strategic issues), the structure of the retreat (e.g., duration; attendance; whether to use breakout groups, and if so, what groups to employ), and the blow-by-blow agenda. Typically headed by the board president and including the superintendent and two or three other board members, the ad hoc committee works closely with the retreat facilitator, who after interviewing committee members and reviewing pertinent documentation (such as last year's retreat report) recommends the key design elements.

The ad hoc committee usually meets only once, either face to face or via teleconference, to review and approve the facilitator's design recommendations, putting in place a detailed retreat "architecture" intended to ensure success and to lower the risk of the event's falling apart to virtually zero. In addition to providing input in generating the detailed retreat design, such ad hoc committees have proved to be useful vehicles for building board member ownership of the retreat, creating, in effect, an influential group of champions for the event who have had an opportunity to bond with the facilitator.

Professional Facilitation

In my experience, a professional facilitator can make three important contributions to the success of your district's retreat: (1) bringing experience of what works and doesn't work to the design process (e.g., how to structure a vision exercise or particular breakout groups); (2) keeping participants on track, ensuring that the retreat objectives are achieved fully within the time allotted in the design; and (3) assisting in the follow-through process, especially producing the follow-up action report. Just imagine seven headstrong board members and several administrators spending a whole day or two together discussing highly complex issues on which there are diverse viewpoints, and you can easily see why self-facilitation would be a risky course of action. Professional facilitators are normally seen as objective participants with no particular axes to grind, giving them a leg up on the superintendent or any other senior administrators who might be tapped to facilitate the retreat. Professional facilitators widely recognized as authorities in areas such as strategic planning and governance also tend to command the respect of retreat participants, who are willing to cede authority for the day or two they spend together.

Retaining the right facilitator is one of the most important retreat design decisions your organization will be making, and so I strongly recommend that this be the initial assignment to your ad hoc retreat design committee. The "retreat from hell" horror stories that I hear all the time are usually the result of choosing the wrong facilitator. In making this critical decision, an organization should review credentials, check references, and even interview candidates for the job. Of course, it would make sense for the superintendent to do quite a bit of the legwork, but the ad hoc committee should seriously consider the decision. Understanding the specific methodologies that facilitators employ is a major part of making the right decision. For example, if you will be holding a full-scale strategic planning retreat that includes updating your organization's values and vision statement, you cannot find the right facilitator without understanding how candidates define values and vision statements and the processes they use to generate them. Otherwise, you just might end up with the whole group wasting a morning wordsmithing a paltry paragraph.

Breakout Groups

Well-designed breakout groups can make a powerful contribution to the success of your retreat. For example, I recently participated in a retreat involving nine breakout groups—three groups meeting concurrently in each of three rounds over the course of one and a half days (in round one, for example, the three groups were values and vision; conditions and trends; and assessment of strengths and weaknesses). Breaking participants into smaller groups is not only a surefire way to foster active participation and, consequently, feelings of ownership, it is also a proven vehicle for generating lots of content. In my experience, the following guidelines will help ensure that the breakout group process is both productive and satisfying:

- Assign board members to lead breakout groups, thereby providing them with ego satisfaction and turning them into strong champions in following through on the retreat. A different board member should lead each group in order to widen board ownership.
- Make sure that the breakout group leaders are well prepared to play their leadership role. You certainly would not want one or more of your colleagues on the board to suffer public embarrassment from fumbling the leader's job in front of board and executive team colleagues. Keep in mind that some of the board members being tapped for the leader's role might never have facilitated a breakout group—or at least the particular ones they will be leading—meaning they will need orientation and training to ensure their success.
- Carefully assign participants to the various groups, making sure not only that each group is as diverse as possible but also that both interest and expertise are taken into account. For example, if one of

your board members has been a prominent advocate of visioning as a strategic tool, you would probably want to make her a member of the vision breakout group. And it would make good sense to involve your district's chief financial officer in the breakout group that discusses financial performance.

- Have every member of every breakout group participate in reporting out in the plenary session, rather than having the leader or a reporter make the group's report. For one thing, this will focus participants' minds on the work of their group (knowing they will have to help present the results in the plenary session); for another, it will make the meeting more interesting and ego satisfying.

Avoid Premature Formal Consensus

School board members, superintendents, and senior managers naturally tend to like closure, and they get pretty uncomfortable when lots of loose ends are left dangling. So every ad hoc retreat design group I have worked with over the years has included at least one board member who argues passionately for a retreat design that results in formal consensus on particular products such as a vision statement or a list of strategic issues. I always strongly counsel against giving in to this natural appetite for certainty because of the harm premature formal consensus, much less firm decision making, can cause. Think about it for a minute. You and your colleagues are spending a relatively brief time together grappling with very complex matters that affect the long-term success of your school system and defy easy understanding, and you are very unlikely to have on hand the information you need to make definitive judgments. Does it really make sense, under the circumstances, to demand closure?

Several years ago I participated as a staff member in a retreat that taught me firsthand the dangers of seeking closure in a short time. The afternoon of the first day together, breakout groups brainstormed strategic issues in the areas of educational performance, administration and management, and image and external relations. In the plenary session following the breakouts, participants were confronted with fifty to sixty issues recorded on flip-chart sheets taped to the wall. So far so good.

The breakout groups had been amazingly productive and creative in generating rough cuts of really important opportunities and challenges facing the organization. Here is where the retreat veered off course— and ultimately came to grief.

The facilitator informed the group at this point that their job was to determine the top five issues in each of the three categories, result- ing in a list of 15 top-priority issues that the organization could tackle subsequent to the retreat. Without getting into the gory details, I will just say that—armed with sticky dots—participants went through an elaborate voting process that did, indeed, result in the identification of the "highest priority" 15 issues. However, the illusion of precision didn't last long after the retreat, as second, third, and fourth thoughts were considered, and within six weeks, the list had bitten the dust. Not only, as it turns out, was precious time wasted in the retreat, but also what could have been an exciting and energizing discussion of is- sues became a tense voting exercise guaranteed to extinguish what- ever good feeling the breakout group brainstorming had generated.

Follow-Through

Building a formal follow-through process into your retreat design can ensure that your organization ultimately realizes a powerful return on your investment of time, energy, and money in the retreat. It also saves you from having to reach premature consensus. Take the previous exam- ple of the retreat that needlessly veered off course because of a poor de- sign incorporating a forced consensus process. The disaster could easily have been averted by building into the retreat design the following steps that many organizations have taken to avoid the illusion of precision:

- The 50 or so issues that the breakout groups generated, and the points made during the following plenary session discussion, are faithfully recorded in their full, rough form, without any attempt at editing other than to correct obvious mistakes.
- A special issue analysis task force consisting of senior administra- tors meets four times over the next 3 months, coming up with a re- fined list of strategic issues that is sent to the superintendent and his or her administrative team, who further refine the list before

sending it to the board's planning committee for review. So loose ends are tied, decisions are made, and action is taken—not prematurely but through a well thought out process.

A CLOSING WORD ON BUDGET AS A CHANGE VEHICLE

In chapter 1, I described the work of a task force that came up with some very practical and affordable ways to involve school board members more proactively and creatively in the annual operational planning and budget preparation process. You might recall that one of the task force's more important recommendations was that an annual prebudget work session be held, involving the board, superintendent, and senior administrators. Your board and superintendent can turn such a work session into an effective innovation and change tool through the following:

- Making sure that the updated vision statement and the operational issues identified in the retreat that kicks off the planning cycle every year are provided to all administrators as input into their operational planning and budget preparation process.
- Asking senior administrators to include in their presentations at the prebudget work session specific planned innovation initiatives responding to specific operational issues, highlighting significant expenditure increases that might be required to implement the initiatives. For example, let's say that one of several operational issues identified at your district's last kickoff retreat was the growing incidence of violence at athletic events. Both your district's athletic director and its director of security would naturally be expected to respond to this issue in their presentations, laying out their planned innovation initiatives to deal with the issue in their respective areas.
- Making sure that discussion of planned innovation initiatives is a key part of the prebudget session (which means setting aside enough time for such discussion, as well as making sure it takes place).
- Ensuring that the ultimate board review of your superintendent's recommended operational plan and budget pays attention to those parts of the budget relating to the innovation initiatives discussed in the prebudget session.

Of course, operational planning and budgeting will always be largely an incremental planning exercise that is essentially administrative in nature, but the simple steps I have just outlined can achieve the twin purposes of upgrading board involvement and fostering innovation and change in your district.

4

HABIT 4: PAY CLOSE ATTENTION TO THE BOARD–SUPERINTENDENT PARTNERSHIP

PRECIOUS BUT OH-SO-FRAGILE

The evidence is in. High-impact school boards that provide their districts with the kind of leadership that makes a real difference in these challenging times never go it alone. They always work in close partnership with their superintendents, as members of a true strategic leadership team. As close collaborators, your board and superintendent make sure that you and your board colleagues play a meaningful role in the governing process, basically by defining your board's governing work in detail and by mapping out the governing structure and processes that you need to do the work. And you and your board colleagues work with your superintendent as a cohesive team in making the judgments and decisions that promote student success and keep your district on a sound footing—financially, administratively, and politically. Your school system's success is proof positive of a true board–superintendent team at work.

But you and your board colleagues should keep in mind that, no matter how strong your board's partnership with your superintendent might appear at any given time, you cannot afford to take it for granted. Human relationships are always fragile, and this one is no exception; indeed, the forces working against a healthy board–superintendent partnership are

daunting. For one thing, today's volatile environment—socially, econom-
ically, politically—bombards your board and superintendent with a neverending stream of complex issues: the change challenges I discussed in
chapter 3. Grappling with them can, over time, cause enough stress and
strain to seriously fray this most precious partnership.

I witnessed firsthand the toll that responding to dramatic demographic change in a community could take on its school district's
board–superintendent partnership. Population loss combined with a
steady increase in childless households forced the district to close
some much-beloved neighborhood elementary schools. The exhausting round of neighborhood meetings at which the superintendent and
board members participated, along with several school board meetings packed with concerned and often angry parents, wore out the relationship over a period of three years, leading to the departure of a
highly capable superintendent whose line of credit with the board
had hit rock bottom. Neither the superintendent nor any board
members did anything wrong; indeed, both parties did a credible job
of leading the district through this excruciatingly difficult time. But,
in retrospect, the lack of attention to keeping the partnership healthy
during a period of tremendous stress allowed it to erode past the
point of saving.

I have also seen board–superintendent partnerships bite the dust because of board member frustration and irritation resulting from dissatisfaction with the board's governing role. Of course, as a school board
member, if you are not involved in doing really high-impact governing
work, you would have to be a saint not to question whether your superintendent is "board savvy" enough to provide you with the support you
need to function at peak governing capacity. Even worse, you would be
justified in asking whether your superintendent even cares much about
developing your board into a high-impact governing body.

Allowing your superintendent's individual CEO leadership priorities and targets to get out of sync with the performance expectations
you and your board colleagues have for your superintendent can be a
real relationship killer if timely action is not taken to bring expectations into alignment. I am constantly surprised at how often this dangerous expectations gap is allowed to develop and to undermine the
board–superintendent partnership to the point where this most pre-

cious of professional marriages cannot be saved, principally because superintendent-specific performance targets are not even discussed—at least not systematically and formally. Countless times I have observed school boards making clear to a brand new superintendent that they want him or her to tackle certain high-priority, clearly defined targets. For example, the board might articulate to its new superintendent that it wants student performance significantly elevated at particular grade levels or in a particular building, that it wants the new superintendent to focus on rebuilding faculty morale districtwide, or that the superintendent should pay special attention to upgrading the board's role in the annual budget preparation process.

But as time passes, and the original expectations have been fulfilled, many board–superintendent teams fail to continue the process of formally negotiating superintendent-specific leadership targets, allowing a dangerous expectations gap to develop. Indeed, I have seen superintendents resist discussing their own individual leadership targets, mistakenly believing that this is a matter of CEO prerogatives and thus outside the pale for board involvement. As you have probably learned by now in your school board career, or through your service on other public and nonprofit boards, a superintendent can feel that things are going great in the district while oblivious to the fact that many if not all board members are feeling dissatisfied with his or her CEO performance. The relationship rupture that often results can be a brutal surprise to the oblivious superintendent.

THE HIGH COST OF A DYSFUNCTIONAL PARTNERSHIP

The easiest course of action for you as a school board member is to take the partnership with your superintendent for granted, but your district, along with you and the other members of the strategic leadership team, will very likely pay a high price as this precious relationship erodes. I strongly believe that you and the colleagues making up your school board are professionally (and morally, to my way of thinking) obligated to do anything you can within reason to keep this most important professional marriage healthy and long lasting. Just think a minute about the toll that will be exacted if the relationship is allowed to erode and eventually dissolve, a situation that is unfortunately quite common in school districts around the country:

- Easily the most important negative consequence of dysfunction at the top in a school district is the failure to make the kind of strategic and policy-level decisions requiring close board–superintendent collaboration in a full and timely fashion, or perhaps not at all. I saw this happen not long ago in a district facing a serious deficit four years or so down the road. A major catastrophe was in the making if some really tough decisions were not made within six months or so, but the frayed board–superintendent partnership, characterized by mutual suspicion and distrust, got in the way of decisive action at every step. Bogged down in endless, often acrimonious debate, the members of this leadership team could not decide on a menu of actions fast enough to avert the inevitable crisis. Rather than carefully cutting back costs and putting an operating levy on the ballot early enough to generate sufficient income, an already frayed leadership team found itself dealing with inevitable cuts in popular programs (such as an outstanding theater arts curriculum) and in administrative and faculty positions, and the team finally reached the point of divorce.

- Your district's image in the community and its relationships with key stakeholders can also be the victims of a dysfunctional board–superintendent partnership. For one thing, relationship failure at the top is likely to confirm to many residents what they already suspected (a widespread belief in this country, unfair or not): your district is not capable of leading and managing itself and thus cannot be expected to serve the best interests of both students and taxpayers. Allowing your board–superintendent partnership to erode plays into the hands of critics, lending credence to the arguments that external (federal and state) pressure is required for public school systems to get their act together and that competition from private, and even for-profit, institutions is the only surefire way to shape up the public schools. And, of course, when such key stakeholders as local government, the chamber of commerce, and service organizations such as Rotary see a school board and superintendent feuding, they are going to be reluctant to support district initiatives, such as a capital construction tax levy.

- The internal management consequences of allowing your board–superintendent partnership to erode or even dissolve can be quite serious. For example, your superintendent's CEO credibility will inevitably erode as he or she fails to get routine matters approved at board meetings, much less deal with the really big issues. In such a situation, your superintendent's capacity to lead internal change will be seriously compromised. Feuding at the top is also a surefire way to dampen employee morale, lessening enthusiasm and commitment. The price might be difficult to quantify, but you can be sure that it will be steep. I recall interviewing administrators a few years ago in a school district whose superintendent was involved in a running battle with the school board. The superintendent had appointed several key administrators to serve on a series of task forces charged to come up with significant improvements in various areas of district management, such as building maintenance, financial planning, personnel management, and contract administration. An overwhelming majority of the administrators I talked with echoed what one person told me: "Confidentially, I'm not about to bust my butt on this task force, coming up with recommendations that [the superintendent] won't be able to get through the board; in fact, I doubt that he'll even be around when the time comes to run them through the board. Sure, I'll participate, but you won't see any of the task forces burning up the track!"

- Finally, as a school board member, you owe it to yourself not to add the pain and suffering that inevitably accompanies a troubled relationship with your superintendent to an already challenging governing role. You would not want to experience what I recently saw at the meeting of a school board at odds with its superintendent (unless, that is, you are a card-carrying masochist): interminable, often strident, and decidedly uncivil debate that produced virtually no resolution; a level of distrust that meant small matters on the agenda were scrutinized down to dotting i's and crossing t's; and a five-hour marathon meeting that ended at midnight, leaving everyone exhausted and depressed.

KEEPING THE MARRIAGE HEALTHY

You and your school board colleagues can take six steps to ensure that the precious professional marriage between your board and superintendent is productive and lasting, generating the high-impact governing that these challenging times demand, while also withstanding the inevitable stress and strains that accompany serious leadership work. You cannot expect to take these steps on your own; your superintendent and senior administrators must be active partners, but you must play an active, leading role in the process, rather than merely sitting back and counting on administrators to bear the full burden of relationship building. Following are the six steps:

1. Make a firm marriage vow, committing to persevere in relationship maintenance through thick and thin.
2. Make sure your superintendent is truly a board-savvy CEO.
3. Assign responsibility for keeping the board–superintendent relationship healthy to a board standing committee.
4. Annually negotiate CEO-specific leadership targets with your superintendent.
5. Regularly—and rigorously—evaluate your superintendent's performance as your district's CEO, making sure that relationship issues are discussed and that the process generates a plan for dealing with the superintendent's performance shortfalls.
6. Stay in close touch with your superintendent.

Make a Firm Marriage Vow

I interviewed several school board members recently in preparation for a two-day retreat involving the board, superintendent, and senior administrators. The superintendent had made me aware of some serious relationship issues, and after talking with the seven board members individually, I understood why the issues might be difficult to fix. In response to being asked what steps the board was taking to keep its partnership with the superintendent positive and solid, four of the seven made very clear to me that they did not see this as the board's worry. Unfortunately, this hands-off attitude is not all that uncommon among board members, in my experience, for two main reasons:

1. Many school board members bring a constituency representation mindset to the boardroom, feeling more committed to dealing with the needs and interests of particular constituencies than to the concept of the board as a "corporate" governing entity. This anti-team attitude obviously militates against the idea of the board's collective accountability for building a solid working relationship with its superintendent, or even governing for that matter. My guess is that this essentially legislative view of school boards is basically the result of their being elected; it is certainly true of city councils and other elected governing bodies, which tend not to work together naturally as cohesive teams, and far less true of appointed or self-appointed boards.

2. The inherently adversarial and limited view of the school board as basically responsible for "watching the critters so they don't steal the store," which probably also comes with the legislative turf, is still fairly common, in my experience. If you and your board colleagues see your role primarily in terms of standing back and judging administrative performance, then the idea of taking the initiative to build a solid partnership with your superintendent will feel alien. After all, adversaries are not naturally partners, not without a lot of hard work.

The high-impact school boards I have observed over the years consciously, explicitly, and formally take responsibility for building and maintaining a productive and positive professional partnership with their superintendents, often by incorporating this commitment into the board's governing mission (see chapter 2). For example, one board's governing mission includes the following element: "Our board plays an active role in making sure that our working relationship with our superintendent is carefully managed in order to keep it sound." Formally adopting a governing mission containing such a clear commitment to playing an affirmative role in partnership building is certainly an important step in the right direction for your board. Of course, such a rhetorical commitment will mean little unless your board actually "walks the talk" by making sure that relationship maintenance structure and processes are established and that substantial board member time is allocated to making them work.

Make Sure You Have a Board-Savvy Superintendent

It takes two to do the partnership tango, and at the heart of every really solid board–CEO working relationship I have observed over the years, including school boards and their superintendents, is a CEO who is truly what I call board savvy. You will know a board-savvy superintendent by his or her (1) positive attitude toward the board, (2) commitment to playing a leading role in building board governing capacity, and (3) knowledge and expertise in the governing "business." First and foremost, the board-savvy superintendent sees the school board as a precious asset to be deployed fully on behalf of the educational mission of the district. The board-savvy superintendent is not defensive in dealings with the board and definitely does not see working with the board as a damage-control challenge. Unfortunately, to judge from the questions I continue to hear from audiences of superintendents around the country, the damage-control philosophy is far from dead, and many superintendents see a large part of their CEO job as keeping their boards from meddling in matters more properly left to the professional educators and administrators.

The really board-savvy superintendents whom I have observed invariably make building their board's capacity to do high-impact governing one of their highest CEO priorities. In practice, this means they do not sit back and wait for the board to get itself together as a governing body; nor do they sit around bemoaning the fact that they are stuck with less than qualified board members doing less than stellar governing work. On the contrary, they are on a mission to help their boards get better in every way at governing, even if this means employing some circuitous strategies. For example, I worked with a superintendent who devoted considerable time and energy during his 1st year in the CEO position to getting his new board to make a commitment to updating its governing performance. His first critical step was to enlist his board president as a governing "change champion" and ally in getting other board members to join them on the board development bandwagon.

Having agreed to lead the board development effort, this board-savvy superintendent's president took the initiative in hosting breakfast and lunch meetings with her colleagues on the board over a 3-month period. At these casual get-togethers, which included the superintendent, the board president took the lead in discussing why it was important for the board to work closely with the superintendent to update its governing role, process, and structure and made clear that this was one of her highest priorities as presiding officer of the board. The superintendent had made a real effort to educate his president on the key ingredients of high-impact governing in preparation for these meetings so that the president would be the up-front leader. The upshot is that the board president appointed a task force involving the superintendent and three of the seven board members to study advances in the field of school governance, assess the board's developmental needs, and come up with some practical enhancements. The board-savvy superintendent provided strong support to the task force, whose efforts really did bear fruit in terms of higher-impact board performance.

Board-savvy superintendents understand the highly complex and rapidly changing field of public and nonprofit governance inside out; otherwise, they could not possibly play a leading role in board capacity building. They are avid students of the governing "business," taking the time and trouble to become real experts by reading the literature and participating in educational programs, rather than merely taking the word of consultants selling one governing flavor or another. I can easily spot a board-savvy superintendent in an audience by the questions he or she asks. For example, I heard the following question recently that could only have come from a truly board-savvy school district CEO: "Dr. _____'s book argues strongly against the use of standing committees, saying that they work against board cohesion and dilute board collective accountability, but you claim that they can be strong 'governing engines.' As far as I can tell from my reading, committees are a hotly debated subject in the field. Would you explain why you think Dr. _____ is wrong in his view, and how my board can manage to have committees without threatening their collective accountability?"

You can use the superintendent evaluation process (covered later in this chapter) as a tool to assess how board savvy your superintendent is, identifying gaps in knowledge and expertise that you can ask your superintendent to fill. The bad news is that many superintendents need considerable work in this area; the good news is that anyone who has reached the top position in a school district is capable of becoming more board savvy if he or she really wants to. One of your jobs as a school board member is to encourage your superintendent to want to. And if you are looking for a new superintendent, you can make "board savvy-ness" one of the search criteria.

This isn't the place for a comprehensive discussion of superintendent recruitment. The point I want to make is that in addition to the standard attributes and qualifications your school board will look for in a new su-perintendent, you want to make sure the candidate's philosophical and operational views on governing and on the board–superintendent part-nership are in sync with the board's. To be blunt, if a board hires a su-perintendent who is worried more about defending executive preroga-tives from meddling board members than about helping the board realize its potential as a governing body, then board capacity building will become a frustrating battleground rather than a matter of creative board–superintendent collaboration.

Making sure the board and its potential superintendent are in sync re-quires, first, that board members actually understand what they are looking for in this regard (otherwise, synchronization is impossible) and, second, that the matter be explored in depth during the interviewing and reference checking. Not addressing this matter during the recruit-ment and selection process can doom the partnership from the get-go.

To take a real-life example, a decade or so ago a school board had found a superintendent candidate who appeared perfect for the job— articulate and polished at the lectern, highly knowledgeable on educa-tional issues, and a master of key functions such as strategic planning, curriculum development, capital planning, financial management, and the like. But during the interview process, no one had taken the trouble to ask probing questions about his views on the governing function and the board–superintendent partnership. It did not appear necessary; af-ter all, he had never run into trouble with a board before, so far as they could tell, and he really seemed to enjoy interacting with board mem-bers during the interview process.

Only during this superintendent's 2nd year on the job did serious ten-sion develop in the relationship, as a majority of board members grew committed to the board's becoming a higher-impact governing body that engaged its members more proactively and creatively in decision mak-ing. Confronted with the demand that he provide assistance in helping the board make this critical transition, the superintendent showed his true colors. Retreating behind a barrier of formal "we–they" ends and means policies (essentially rules), he resisted in every way possible short of outright defiance any deeper board involvement in strategic decision making or the implementation of a stronger standing committee structure. His idea of partnership, as it turned out, was a black and white division of labor between the board's ends-focused work and the staff's means-focused functions. The break eventually came, but at a high cost that might have been prevented by asking the right questions during the recruitment process.

Experience has taught me that board members' being very direct, listening carefully, and asking follow-up questions to clarify points is the ticket to determining whether there is a close enough philosophical fit to support and sustain a positive working relationship over the long run. For example, here are some important questions that discerning board members have asked their potential superintendents in the area of governance and the board–superintendent partnership. Keep in mind that this is only a sampling, and for each question there might be a number of follow-up questions.

- We are really interested in being a high-impact governing board that makes a significant difference in the affairs of our district. What, in your experience, are the characteristics of a truly effective school board? More specifically, would you describe the governing role and governing work of such a board?
- Would you describe how you helped your last board build its capacity to govern more effectively?
- What concrete steps might you take as our superintendent to help us become a higher-impact governing body?
- Can you think of any barriers that might get in the way of developing our governing capacity, and how do you think we might deal with them?
- Taking the areas of strategic planning and annual budget preparation, at what particular points—and exactly how—do you think the board should be involved?
- In your experience, what are the characteristics of a really positive and productive board–superintendent working relationship?

- What steps can you take as our superintendent to make sure our working relationship remains healthy?
- What are the characteristics of an effective process for board evaluation of superintendent performance?

Of course, you will also want to make sure that your reference checking process includes probing questions intended to determine how board savvy your candidate is. There is no reason why your superintendent search committee would not contact two or three of the past school board presidents that the candidate worked with, asking in-depth questions about the candidate's board development philosophy and initiatives; how the candidate involved the board in strategic planning, budgeting, and performance monitoring; what kind of superintendent performance evaluation process was employed; and the like.

Employ a Standing Committee

As I have already pointed out more than once in this book, if you and your board colleagues want to make sure that your school board fully executes well-designed leadership processes (such as the board's involvement in innovation and change activities), it makes sense to employ standing committees to participate in designing the processes and to take the lead in executing them. This is certainly true of the complex and high-stakes process of building and maintaining your board's partnership with your superintendent, which demands the kind of in-depth attention that the regular monthly board meeting cannot possibly provide and which would not be appropriate for the president of your board to handle on behalf of his or her board colleagues.

Accordingly, many boards have chosen to utilize a standing executive (or governance) committee, typically consisting of the board president, the other standing committee chairs, and the superintendent, to handle the board–superintendent working relationship. In this capacity, the executive committee does the following:

- Makes sure the superintendent's position description is updated periodically
- Negotiates CEO-specific performance targets with the superintendent

- Monitors the board–superintendent relationship continuously, identifying issues that have developed and working with the superintendent to resolve them (or preventing emerging issues from becoming full blown), with special attention to board–superintendent communication since that is a frequent trouble spot in today's turbulent environment
- At least annually conducts an in-depth evaluation of superintendent performance, resulting in a game plan for addressing identified performance shortfalls
- Negotiates the superintendent's compensation package and recommends its adoption to the full board

Negotiate CEO-Specific Leadership Targets

Earlier in this chapter I suggested that allowing a gap to develop between the superintendent's and board's views of the superintendent's CEO-specific performance targets is a surefire way to erode this most precious and fragile of partnerships. A reliable way to prevent this from happening is to make sure your board's executive committee annually negotiates a detailed set of what I call CEO-specific performance targets with your superintendent and to make these targets a primary part of the committee's annual evaluation of superintendent performance (discussed later in the chapter). In developing this set of targets, your executive committee and superintendent will answer the following question: What specific targets should the superintendent, as our district's CEO, devote significant individual time and attention to achieving in the coming year? In other words, what unique value will the superintendent add to district affairs, beyond overall leadership and administration of the district?

The point of negotiating specific CEO targets—above and beyond the district's overall targets related to student achievement, finances, administration, and the like that are established through the annual operational planning and budget process—is to provide your board and superintendent with a more finely calibrated instrument to employ in both assessing the superintendent's performance as CEO and managing the relationship. This is critical to maintaining a healthy partnership for the very simple reason that board–CEO relationships reach the breaking point every day in organizations, including school districts, that are generally performing well according to the districtwide performance targets set through the planning process. Countless times over the past 25 years I have seen CEOs, including a number of superintendents, receive high marks for overall leadership of their organizations while at the same time running into serious relationship trouble with their boards, over such CEO-specific matters as support for the board in developing its governing capacity, how the external relations role is divided between the board and superintendent, and board–CEO communication.

I want to be clear that I am not suggesting your superintendent's CEO-specific leadership targets are as important in the grand scheme of things as the bottom-line educational and administrative targets your superintendent and senior administrators develop through the annual operational planning and budget process and you and your board colleagues ultimately adopt. Nor do I believe your superintendent's CEO-specific targets need to be uniformly quantitative since that would be unrealistic in the area of CEO leadership. The point is to employ a tool that enables you and your board colleagues to engage in a creative, detailed discussion with your superintendent about his or her leadership role and to decide how to go about assessing superintendent leadership in a meaningful fashion, with the ultimate aim of maintaining a close, productive, and healthy partnership.

Your board's reaching agreement with the superintendent on a set of CEO-specific performance targets for the coming year can be a straightforward process. First, agree on the categories within which the targets will be developed. Second, have your superintendent develop a set of targets in these performance categories. Third, spend adequate time discussing the targets with your superintendent and then formally adopting them as one of two sets of evaluation criteria (the other set being the overall district performance targets set through the planning process). In my experience, four categories of CEO-specific performance make up a workable framework:

1. The board–superintendent partnership: including superintendent support for the board in carrying out its governing work; board capacity building; board–superintendent communication

2. External relations: including representation of the district to the public at large and in particular forums in the community; relationships with particular community stakeholders; media relations
3. Strategic planning and innovation and change: including how the board will be involved in the innovation and change process; what innovation and change issues and initiatives will receive intensive superintendent attention
4. Internal management and administration: specific improvements in internal management and administration that the superintendent will focus significant individual time on; specific issues that the superintendent will take the lead in solving

Looking at these four categories, you can easily see that they provide a workable framework for discussing the CEO work of your superintendent and for grappling with potential and actual issues that are both pertinent to the board–superintendent partnership and that would not likely come up in the normal operational planning process of your district. For example, here are some targets that boards and superintendents have reached agreement on over the years:

- Regarding the board–superintendent partnership, I, as your superintendent, will in the coming year
  - make sure the board's three new standing committees become fully functional
  - upgrade my communication with the board by implementing a biweekly e-mail update for the board and making sure that I meet with every board member individually for an hour every month
  - work closely with the treasurer to improve the monthly financial report, making it easier to understand by adding an executive summary and employing bar charts comparing actual with budget expenditures by major functional areas—monthly and year to date
- Regarding external relations, I, as your superintendent, will in the coming year
  - make sure the board speakers bureau is fully implemented, ensuring that every board member is booked to speak in a least one

community forum every quarter and is provided with an attractive PowerPoint presentation to use in making the presentation
- pay special attention to rebuilding our district's working relationship with the mayor's office and city council by improving communication generally and, more specifically, by making sure they are regularly briefed on important educational issues
- see that our district finds a seat at the economic development table, specifically that both a board member and I are invited to serve on the newly created community economic development task force
- Regarding strategic planning and innovation and change, I, as your superintendent, will in the coming year
  - make sure faculty members are well represented on the task forces being created to come up with change initiatives to address the strategic issues we identified at the last retreat
  - play a hands-on role in putting the capital levy steering committee together, making sure that it represents every major sector and key stakeholders in our community and that it is provided with a clear charge and adequate executive support
- In the area of management and administration, I, as your superintendent, will in the coming year
  - make sure the new director of contract management position is filled with a highly qualified candidate and that new policies and procedures are developed and put into place by June 30
  - play a hands-on leadership role in addressing the issue of internal morale, making sure the employee survey that will be conducted in September indicates significant improvement in every measurement category

Of course, your superintendent's CEO-specific performance targets in these four key executive areas will provide a more solid foundation for your board's evaluation of superintendent performance (see the next section) to the extent that they can be quantified. Even though this will not always be possible, trying to come up with measurable indicators that the performance promises are being kept will add objectivity to the evaluation process. For example, referring back to the previous examples, the target to "make sure the board's three new standing committees become fully functional" can be measured by defining what "fully functional" means: That each committee must be thoroughly oriented on its responsibilities? That each committee is meeting at least monthly? That each committee is reporting on its work at regular board meetings?

You will not be surprised to learn that some superintendents will not welcome a dialogue with their school boards on their CEO-specific leadership targets, viewing it from a traditional defensive perspective as an assault on executive prerogatives. Time and again, when I mention the subject in presentations to state K–12 administrator associations, I see skeptical looks on several faces in the audience, and several hands shoot up to challenge me. The inevitable remark goes something like this: "My board's job isn't to do my job! How I use my time doing X, Y, and Z isn't any of their business. I'm paid to be the CEO; I'll do the job my way, and they can just judge the bottom-line results. That's what a board is for. If I get them involved in discussing my detailed leadership work, the next thing I know they'll be sitting in my chair and lobbing commands to my senior administrative team. No thank you!"

My response is a dose of tough love: "I feel your pain, dear colleagues; I know the idea sends chills up and down your spines. But you've got no choice if you really want to have a strong, mutually satisfying relationship with your school board. Reaching detailed agreement with your board on your individual leadership targets is the surest way to avert the issues that can kill the partnership, no matter how well your district is performing overall. By participating in such a dialogue, you make it possible to discuss matters, such as your board members' ego satisfaction, that would otherwise fall through the cracks and come back to haunt you. And you also convey your fundamental executive maturity and self-confidence by enabling the dialogue."

Tackle the Big Kahuna: Superintendent Evaluation

No tool is more powerful than regular, formal school board evaluation of superintendent performance in maintaining a healthy board–superintendent working relationship. Unfortunately, many if not most school boards do a less than effective job of carrying out their evaluation responsibility. Some boards have been known to leave superintendent evaluation to the board president, thereby abdicating their collective responsibility; others have relied on one of those generic checklists that measure functional competence (e.g., assessing how well the superintendent handles long-range financial planning) while ignoring critical leadership outcomes. And I have encountered school boards that have gone for years without evaluating their superintendents' performance, either because they do not recognize the importance of evaluation as a leadership tool, feel uncomfortable judging their superintendents, or just plain do not know how to go about evaluating performance.

Although a well-designed superintendent evaluation process can be very helpful in making judgments about your superintendent's compensation level, making a very sensible link between performance and financial rewards, the primary objective of the process is to strengthen superintendent performance and the board–superintendent partnership. The following design features are characteristic of evaluation processes that fully achieve these aims:

- A board standing committee takes explicit responsibility for developing the detailed design of the evaluation process and for conducting the evaluation. If your school board has fewer than seven members, then it will make sense for the whole board to conduct the evaluation, sitting as a committee of the whole. Either way, intensive time is set aside to do the evaluation outside of the regular board meeting framework.
- In carrying out the evaluation, the responsible committee employs two sets of criteria for assessing superintendent performance:
  1. Overall district performance targets, as defined through the operational planning and budget preparation process
  2. Superintendent CEO-specific targets (see the preceding section) that are negotiated with the superintendent
- The process involves intensive, face-to-face committee–superintendent dialogue, making the superintendent an active participant in the evaluation and never leaving him or her out of the loop. Issues relating to the board–superintendent partnership, no matter how sensitive, are explicitly addressed during this dialogue, which might require two or more committee meetings over a period of weeks.

- Going beyond the performance appraisal itself, the evaluation process results in detailed agreement between the committee and superintendent on the specific steps the superintendent will take during the coming year to correct performance shortfalls and clear deadlines for each step.
- The committee briefs the full board on its evaluation and the resulting superintendent plan of corrective action in an executive session.

Stay in Close Touch

There is not much new under the sun that I can say about the subject of board–superintendent communication, which is obviously a vital component of any human relationship involving close collaboration and teamwork. The most important counsel I can share is to make sure the standing committee to which you and your board colleagues have assigned the responsibility of maintaining the board–superintendent partnership pays constant, close attention to board–superintendent communication. This means monitoring communication, assessing its effectiveness, identifying problems, and reaching agreement with the superintendent on practical steps that might be taken to strengthen communication.

Let me bring this brief discussion to a close by suggesting a five-point school board "bill of rights" in the communications area, detailing what you deserve and should expect from your superintendent and senior administrators:

1. *You and your board colleagues should be kept current on pertinent issues.*
   Being kept abreast of important developments in the fields of K–12 education and public and nonprofit governance is quite pertinent to your leadership work as a school board member, providing a context and framework for strategic and policy-level decision making. Your superintendent is well positioned to keep you up to date on national and state political, regulatory, and legislative matters and on developments in the profession, such as dramatic advances in computer-assisted instruction. This information can be provided in reports at board meetings and through faxed

or e-mailed briefings. Your superintendent might also take the trouble to have someone in his or her office regularly review periodicals, clip pertinent pieces, and circulate them among you and your board colleagues.

2. *You and your board colleagues should be apprised of emerging issues.*

   You should expect to be alerted to emerging issues in your community (e.g., a communitywide task force the chamber of commerce is putting together to come up with strategies to attract new firms) and internally in the school system (e.g., a simmering dispute between several teachers and a new principal at one of your elementary schools) that might require board action at some point in the future, or at least are likely to confront board members through questions from constituents and the media. Allowing board members to be caught off guard and embarrassed because of lack of timely information is, in the world of educational administration, a cardinal sin.

3. *You and your school board colleagues should not have to suffer undue pain in the process of governing.*

   Policy recommendations, performance reports, contract actions, and other paper flowing to you and your board colleagues should be carefully crafted to make your governing deliberations easier and more enjoyable. I am not suggesting that you should expect your governing work to be a lark; but you certainly should expect that it will not entail needless pain and suffering. Such techniques as providing brief executive summaries backed up by detail and taking the trouble to convey financial information in a graphical format (rather than as page after page of forbidding columns and rows of numbers that would challenge a CPA) have made the work of many boards less painful. Many public and nonprofit CEOs these days, including superintendents, are experimenting with the use of audiovisual support in making presentations at committee and board meetings (e.g., employing PowerPoint slides or showing a video).

4. *You and your board colleagues should have frequent informal interaction with your superintendent.*

   You and I both know that distance militates against creative collaboration, and the emotional bonding that comes from close, informal contact facilitates partnership. You should expect that your superintendent will take the initiative in fostering informal interaction among board members, the superintendent, and senior administrators. Many superintendents regularly meet one on one with board members away from the shop, over breakfast or lunch, taking the trouble to get to know their policy makers at a more intimate level. Informal gatherings of board members and administrators can easily be orchestrated (e.g., a regularly scheduled light supper before every board meeting, at which no business is discussed, and social events such as a summer picnic and holiday get-togethers).

5. *You and your board colleagues should receive accurate and complete information.*

   Trust cements partnerships, and you and your board colleagues should be able to trust that whatever you hear or read from your superintendent and senior administrators not only is true but also presents a complete picture, not leaving out any details pertinent to your full understanding. Receiving an unduly rosy report on a major construction project in your district, when there is a clear and present danger of its falling behind and going over budget, would erode trust and be totally unacceptable.

HABIT 5: REACH OUT
EXTERNALLY AND INTERNALLY

A CASE FOR HANDS-ON INVOLVEMENT

Reflect on the definition of governing work proposed in chapter 1: you and your board colleagues playing the leading role in answering—over and over again—three fundamental questions that define your school system now and in the future, in the process helping to shape, and making judgments and decisions about, a variety of governing "products." You will recall that these key questions are (1) where should your school district be headed over the long run? (2) what should your school district be now and in the short run? and (3) how well is your school district performing?

By its very nature, governing is a pretty aloof business accomplished well away from your district's day-to-day operations, and that is the way it should be. In fact, the first and foremost habit of high-impact school boards is that they really do concentrate on their governing work. However, this is not to say that you and your board colleagues should exclusively govern and nothing else. I think a strong case can be made for you to play a hands-on nongoverning role in two areas: reaching out to key constituencies in your community beyond the boundaries of your school system and also playing a visible role in building a positive internal climate within system boundaries. There are two compelling reasons why you and your board colleagues should not limit yourselves to governing. First, you are uniquely qualified to play a diplomatic and political role externally and internally. Second, the need for your active involvement in this nongoverning area is tremendous. The challenge for you as a school board member is to play this political and diplomatic role fully without seriously diluting your fundamental mission: to provide your district with high-impact governing.

These are without question uniquely challenging times for public education. Not only have our public school systems, along with other public organizations and institutions, suffered a dramatic loss of legitimacy and authority over the past 40 years, but our public schools are actually under assault. Granted, public education has always been on the firing line, and criticism is nothing new; however, going back 40 years or so, there was widespread and fundamental trust in our public schools. The average citizen was inclined to take more on faith and to be less distrustful than today. And if not particularly generous in their financial support in many systems, at least not many systems were faced with the challenge of proving they were not mismanaging district affairs and misleading the community.

These days, by contrast, you and your school board colleagues are likely to receive a very different message from many residents in your community, along these lines: "You've got to work for my support, demonstrate why I should trust you, show me what concrete good you're doing, prove that you aren't wasting my hard-earned money." Such public skepticism about both the motives and basic competence of our public schools presents more than an external relations problem that over time will adversely affect school enrollment and financial stability. It also inevitably takes a serious toll on the internal culture of a public school system, generating considerable stress, dampening morale, and lessening commitment. No normal human being could go to work day after day—either to the classroom or administrative office—without being affected by the continuous drumbeat of distrust and criticism.

You and your school board colleagues are in a unique position to make a significant contribution—both through your governing and your hands-on political and diplomatic work—to strengthening your district's public image, building its relationships with critical constituents and stakeholders, and fostering a positive internal climate:

- Your school board position gives you unique visibility and clout; you are not only perceived as an important leader but also viewed as above the fray and less captive to the system you are responsible for governing than the superintendent and other administrators.
- You come to the boardroom with strong community networks and familiarity with the people who elected you and whom you represent on the board. You are of the community, not outside it, and this uniquely equips you to reach out, capturing minds and hearts on behalf of the public schools.

WHAT HIGH-IMPACT SCHOOL BOARDS ARE DOING

High-impact school boards around the country are responding forcibly and creatively to the external and internal relations challenge, through both their governing and hands-on nongoverning work. Success in this realm, in my experience, depends on two critical preconditions:

1. As a school board member you must really want to play an affirmative role in reaching out to the wider community, turning inward to help build a healthy internal culture, and you and your board colleagues must take steps to formalize the commitment. For example, many boards add to their governing mission (see chapter 2) an explicit statement such as "Our board will play an active role in promoting our district's image in the community and positive working relationships with key community constituencies." Participation in community relations activities can also be built into your board members' performance targets, such as "Board members are expected to speak on behalf of our district in selected community forums at least four times a year."
2. Your superintendent and senior administrators must really want you to play this role and be committed to providing you with the support you need to succeed. You and your board colleagues have neither the time nor other resources to do the job alone. This support role will include such activities as collecting information on important speaking opportunities, developing PowerPoint presentations and other materials that board members can use in speaking engagements, and even orchestrating speaker rehearsal sessions.

Wearing their governing hats, the members of a high-impact board are playing a creative role, in partnership with their superintendent and senior administrators, in shaping their district's desired image (how it wants to be perceived by the public at large and by particular stakeholders in the community); adopting strategies to promote the image; monitoring progress in image building and public relations; and in the internal arena, reaching agreement with the superintendent on the highest priority concerns about climate and culture. On the nongoverning front, boards are

- speaking on behalf of their systems in community forums, often employing a formal board speakers bureau
- serving as liaisons with key stakeholder groups in the community
- representing their school board colleagues in internal system events

I must inject a serious caveat here: You can bring only so much time and energy to your school board service, and your preeminent responsibility is to concentrate on doing the kind of high-impact governing work your district always needs. Your public school system cannot afford your becoming so immersed in your nongoverning work that your governing role is diluted. This will always be a clear and present danger for the simple reason that doing nongoverning work tends to be fun and ego satisfying and usually far less stressful than grappling with thorny strategic and policy issues. The surest guard against diluting your governing work is an executive, or governance, committee that actively plans, coordinates, and monitors the board's governing and nongoverning work. Some boards, typically with at least nine members, have created an external stakeholder relations committee to oversee board participation in the external arena, working side by side with the two "meat and potatoes" governing committees: planning and performance oversight.

WEARING YOUR GOVERNING HAT: IMAGE AND STRATEGY FORMULATION

Over the years I have seen many public and nonprofit organizations, including school districts, make three fundamental mistakes in dealing with their constituents and stakeholders:

1. Taking the community for granted, assuming that good works speak for themselves, and hence investing little in image building and external relations. I learned how dangerous this course of action could be almost 20 years ago, when my children's school district lost an operating levy for the first time in almost 40 years. Surveys taken after the election indicated that voters were generally supportive of the school system but felt taken for granted and condescended to. By the way, the levy was passed 6 months later, after the school board and top administrators made a concerted effort to communicate the district's vision and respond to residents' concerns.

2. Taking action on the public relations front only when needing extraordinary support (e.g., wanting an operating levy passed) or responding to a crisis (a highly critical series of articles in the local newspaper; an unexpected deficit calling for Draconian measures). Today's environment of a skeptical, if not downright hostile, public makes this a dangerous course in the best of times. People's attitudes these days are not changed overnight.

3. Taking a shallow approach to public relations, relying on an advertising firm to come up with a new district logo, slogan, and some public service announcements. Such tools might make a small difference, but the level of distrust and suspicion these days is likely to make glib approaches counterproductive, insulting the intelligence of the residents of your community.

In my experience, public school systems that have built a stellar image in their communities and a firm foundation of public support that cannot easily be shaken have invested considerable time, serious thought, and financial resources in community relations. Wearing your governing hat, the most important contribution you can make to your school district's community relations efforts is to play a creative role in shaping—in collaboration with your superintendent and senior administrators—two indispensable governing "products":

1. A detailed district vision statement (see the discussion in chapter 1) that paints a clear picture of long-term district aspirations in terms of impacts on the community, the district's roles, and the values that provide an ethical framework for all district operations

2. A detailed district image statement, describing how you, your board colleagues, the superintendent, and senior administrators want the district to be perceived by the public at large and key stakeholders in your community

Your district's vision statement is intended to be both an internal guide and framework for planning and management and a powerful community education tool. It enables people in your community to understand your school system in more fundamental and inspirational terms than just what its operations cost or the direct experience of parents with children in the system, lifting their sights to fundamental outcomes and guiding values. As I pointed out in the first chapter, many districts make the visioning process a particularly powerful external relations tool by involving community focus groups in shaping the vision statement. It can also be an integral part of a comprehensive communication program, appearing in various district publications and commented on whenever possible in presentations to community groups.

Your district's image statement serves a different purpose: providing you with essential guidance in coming up with the key messages you want to get out to the community and in fashioning community relations strategies. Without knowing—in real detail—how you want your school system to be perceived in the community generally and by particular constituencies and stakeholder groups more specifically, how could you possibly determine the messages your district needs to convey publicly, much less how to convey them? Although your district's image statement plays a key role in fashioning external relations strategies, it is basically an internal tool. Unlike your district's vision statement, it will never be published or explicitly quoted in presentations in community forums. Its presence will be felt indirectly, through your district's community relations efforts.

Before turning to the content of a detailed image statement and how to go about generating one, let me deal with a concern that some readers might have. The problem many board members have with image building is that it can have a manipulative feel, and as a board member dedicated to the educational and social mission of your school district, feeling like a salesperson, rather than a statesperson, is likely to cause some discomfort. I can empathize, but I must counsel you to get over any guilt you might have because it is unfounded. If there is one lesson experience has taught over and over again in the field of public relations it is that good works never speak for themselves—except, perhaps, to the direct beneficiaries of your educational efforts, and even they might not see all that clearly the value your public school system has added to the community. One of your most important contributions to this process, wearing your board governing hat, is to ensure that no significant gap exists between the image your district is conveying and reality. Painting a false picture is immoral and totally unacceptable; anyway, the odds of fooling many people much of the time are nil.

A very effective approach to fashioning a detailed district image is to brainstorm image elements in a board–superintendent–senior administrator retreat, at which a breakout group might fashion the statement by completing the sentence, "We want to be seen as . . ." Subsequently, the image statement might be polished by the superintendent and senior administrators and massaged by the board's external stakeholder relations committee and eventually finalized. Real-life image statements school district leaders have fashioned have included such elements as "doing a top-quality job of educating our students," "welcoming the active involvement of our students' parents," "open and responsive to our community," "making a major contribution to the quality of life in our community," "prudently managing financial and other resources," and "creative partnerships in community economic development."

An updated image statement is your board's primary governing contribution in the community relations arena. With this framework in hand, it is basically up to your superintendent and senior administrators to fashion detailed community relations strategies, with you and your board colleagues now playing a more traditional review and approval mode, perhaps under the leadership of your external/stakeholder relations committee. For example, your superintendent and the district's associate superintendent for public information might come to the committee with a package that includes an updated school district logo and related key messages to be conveyed by various means—through the annual report, in presentations to civic groups, through public service announcements, and via an updated website. Extraordinary proposed expenditures outside of the approved budget—say, for the website enhancements—will, of course, go through the normal review and approval process.

When you review such proposed strategies, one of your key governing responsibilities is to determine whether key elements of your district's image statement are being adequately addressed. For example, examining the key messages the updated website is intended to convey, wearing your governing hat, you and your colleagues on the external stakeholder relations committee might ask, "Are we really getting across the message that our district is making a huge contribution to our community's quality of life and its economic development?" "Is the importance we place on prudently managing the tax dollars we receive being clearly conveyed?"

Wearing your governing hat, you and your board colleagues will also play your normal role of monitoring the execution of community relations strategies, making sure they are producing the planned impacts in the community in terms of improving perceptions of your district and forging stronger relationships with key stakeholders. For example, your external stakeholder relations committee might work with the superintendent and responsible senior administrator to design and execute an annual survey intended to measure community perceptions of your district, or it may decide to employ focus groups to test changing perceptions over the course of the year.

YOUR DISTRICT'S PUBLIC INFORMATION OFFICER

In many if not most school districts, a senior administrator serves as the district "public information officer," in this capacity usually reporting directly to the superintendent or to an associate superintendent. In these challenging times, when people are so skeptical of institutions and image building, and therefore community relations are so critical, your public information officer is an important member of your district's strategic leadership team. Public information officers, in my experience, play three key roles:

1. They serve as chief staff to the board's external community relations committee, making sure the committee is well advised on external community relations strategy and providing assistance to the committee in monitoring external community relations activities.

2. They serve as the district's liaison—and first point of contact—with the print and electronic media. Board members in districts where external relations are well managed routinely refer all media questions to their public relations officer; otherwise, you can imagine the mixed messages that might dilute a district's image-building strategy. This does not mean that, as a school board member, you should not have regular media contact, but it does mean that you should avoid ad hoc contact and, instead, participate in an organized program of media relations staffed by your public information officer.

3. They serve as the superintendent's chief external relations lieutenant, in this capacity scheduling superintendent interviews, drafting presentations, and the like.

A WORD ON STAKEHOLDER RELATIONS

Community relations can be seen as a number of relationships with specific stakeholders in your community, rather than merely public relations generally; the more explicitly your district's strategies are focused on the stakeholder relationships involving the highest stakes, the likelier your district's investment in community relations will yield a powerful return. A stakeholder is a group, organization, or institution—and sometimes even a particular individual—with which your district needs to build and maintain a relationship because something is at stake: diplomatically, politically, financially, technically. Wearing your governing hat, you and your school board colleagues can play a creative role in identifying key stakeholders and the stakes involved in each relationship, ultimately reviewing strategies the superintendent recommends for maintaining the more important relationships.

One of the more productive and entertaining activities in many board–superintendent–senior administrator retreats I have seen is for a breakout group to do a preliminary stakeholder analysis, involving the following steps:

• First make a long list of stakeholders in the community with which it makes sense for your district to maintain some kind of relationship; the list is often amazingly long: office of the mayor, city council, state legislative delegation, local newspaper and other media, chamber of commerce, Rotary and other service organizations, state department of education, the community college, the state school board and administrators associations, and many more.

- Second, identify the stakes involved for the school system in each of the relationships, and select ten to fifteen stakeholders involving the highest stakes.

- Third, for your list, do what I call a "quid pro quo analysis," asking the following for each stakeholder: What does our school district need/want from this particular stakeholder relationship, and what do we think the stakeholder needs/wants in return? For example, take the chamber of commerce, from which our district primarily wants a forum for presenting information on our district's vision and educational programs; recognition of K–12 education's critical role in community and economic development, basically by granting our district a seat at the table when community economic development strategies are being formulated; and strong support for future tax levies. We think that, in return, the chamber needs/wants from our district our membership in—and financial support for—the chamber; active participation of the superintendent in chamber activities; and a willingness to share information on district plans and performance, among other things.

- Fourth, assess each relationship in terms of how close, positive, and productive it is, and identify any relationship problems that stand out. For example, in one stakeholder exercise I was involved in, participants noted that dealings with the mayor's office had become increasingly negative, as evidenced by her highly critical comments to a newspaper reporter recently about the "arrogant and unresponsive" school board.

In my experience, this simple exercise often comes as a revelation to school board members and their administrative colleagues, who are bowled over by both the number of important stakeholders in the community demanding attention and the complexity of the stakes involved. The sheer number of relationships demanding attention makes a compelling case for hands-on involvement by you and your board colleagues in the nongoverning work of stakeholder relationship management, which the superintendent and senior administrators could not possibly handle by themselves.

After the initial list has been generated in the retreat, the key follow-up step is for the superintendent and senior administrators to prepare a detailed strategy for managing each identified relationship as part of the overall community relations strategy formulation process I described previously. Such a strategy typically consists of your district's major objectives vis-à-vis the stakeholder over the coming year (e.g., turning the mayor into a vocally strong ally of the district; getting the mayor's endorsement for our upcoming capital improvements bond issue); the strategies for achieving these objectives (e.g., monthly luncheon meetings involving the mayor, school board president, and superintendent); and a workplan identifying board and administrative responsibilities for carrying out the strategies (e.g., by no later than April 30, the board president will formally invite the mayor to chair the bond issue steering committee). Wearing your governing hat, you and your board colleagues will monitor progress in implementing the stakeholder relations strategies, as part of your normal performance oversight responsibilities.

YOUR NONGOVERNING, HANDS-ON DOING

In my experience, the three most productive strategies for hands-on, nongoverning school board involvement in the external arena are (1) a board speakers bureau, (2) board member facilitation of community forums, and (3) board member participation in maintaining particularly high-priority stakeholder relationships. The board speakers bureau is a simple high-yield approach that can serve your district as a powerful communication vehicle while also providing you and your board colleagues with an enjoyable, ego-satisfying nongoverning experience. Community groups appreciate senior administrators making the effort to address them, but presentations by unpaid board members tend to be much higher impact in terms of relationship building.

Following are key components of bureaus that I have seen work very well in promoting their district's image and public relations:

- Board oversight of the bureau, which is often the responsibility of the board's external/stakeholder relations committee, working closely with the superintendent and the senior administrator with the community relations portfolio (often known as the public information officer). Oversight involves the following:

- Identifying—based on the superintendent's recommendations—top-priority community forums, such as the monthly luncheon meetings of Rotary, women's clubs, and the chamber of commerce

- Enlisting board members to speak and matching them with particular forums

- Reaching agreement on the key messages to be conveyed in presentations (within the framework of your district's updated image statement, which provides broad themes, and varying in specific content with changing district circumstances—for example, needing to pass an operating levy or to explain a particular issue, such as wide variation in standardized test scores among buildings)

- Board member commitment of time and energy to participating, including making the effort to rehearse presentations to ensure their effectiveness. As I mentioned earlier in this chapter, an essential precondition for board member participation is to formally bless such participation by incorporating it into both your board's governing mission and the board member performance standards.

- Strong executive support from your superintendent and senior administrators, such as developing specific presentation points, putting together an attractive PowerPoint presentation for you and your board colleagues to use, providing you and your colleagues with pertinent handout material, and structuring formal rehearsal sessions.

You and some of your board colleagues might not be fond of public speaking; many very capable and experienced leaders are not, in my experience. I make much of my living speaking in public and, even now, contend with a sense of dread before every appearance, keenly aware of—but not paralyzed by—the feeling of potential rejection. However, you do not need to be a charismatic personality or the world's most polished platform speaker to succeed on the podium. Just keep in mind that actually going out there on the hustings with a clear message and good supportive material is perhaps the single most powerful and cost-effective tool you and your board members can wield in fostering positive community relations.

My only caveat is thoroughly rehearse, and then rehearse some more, preferably in a group setting (perhaps with board colleagues and administrators)—going through the slide presentation until you feel entirely comfortable with it. Until standing up and running through the presentation in front of your colleagues, you cannot possibly know how it will sound and feel (well paced? dragging? natural? stilted? not enough elaboration on particular points?). Without adequate rehearsal, you risk sounding awkward and uncomfortable in public, which will reduce your effectiveness as an ambassador for your district. Be assured that once you and your colleagues have made the PowerPoint presentation to three or four groups, you will feel like a real pro at the lectern.

Chairing or facilitating a community forum on behalf of your district can be a powerful image builder and communication tool for your system. You can not only demonstrate publicly that you and your board colleagues really do care about community relations but also communicate your district's openness and responsiveness by inviting the community to participate in important school business. To take a real-life example, a school district successfully involved community members in fleshing out two critical planning products: its values and vision statements. The first-cut statements had been generated in a two-day board retreat and touched up a bit by the superintendent and his senior administrators. At this point, the board's planning committee worked with the superintendent in scheduling three forums around the community, at which residents were invited to comment on the draft statements. Members of the planning committee led these feedback sessions, which proved highly effective at surfacing participants' questions and concerns and generating active discussion.

Building and maintaining relationships with key stakeholders is an immense challenge that your superintendent and senior administrators could not possibly handle without the active, hands-on involvement of you and your board members, wearing your nongoverning, doing hat. Earlier in this chapter, I discussed the key components of an effectively led and managed stakeholder relations program. At this point, I would like to share some examples of productive board member involvement in actually carrying out such a program:

- One of your board members agrees to serve as formal liaison with a particular stakeholder organization, such as the chamber of commerce, in this capacity: actively participating in the stake-holder's affairs (perhaps even serving on the stakeholder board or one or more of its committees); representing your district to the stakeholder, making sure that district activities and positions on particular issues are well understood; and identifying and alerting your school board colleagues and superintendent of stakeholder relationship problems that need to be addressed and playing an active role in working through these problems.

- The local community college president is assembling a task force to look at the development of customized education and training pro-grams that might be packaged and provided to expanding and re-locating businesses in the community, taking advantage of available federal and state vocational/technical education funding. Your school district has been invited to participate, and your school board and superintendent agree that the district should be repre-sented by a two-member team: the district's director of curriculum development and a board member who has been long interested in your district's involvement in economic development. Your board's planning and resource development committee provides the team with guidelines for district involvement and requests that the com-mittee be briefed monthly on task force activities.

- Your district has submitted a grant application to the community foundation, requesting $150,000 to cover the cost of investigating the special needs of students in the dramatically growing Latino population in your community, who are experiencing seriously lag-ging student achievement and a high dropout rate, and of develop-ing and pilot testing special programs to address these needs. Your school board president and chair of the planning and resource de-velopment committee accompany your superintendent and associ-ate superintendent for pupil services to a meeting with the founda-tion CEO and two program officers to discuss the application.

- Several city council members have been vocal critics of your school district over the past few months, raising serious questions about your district's capacity to manage its finances and suggesting that tax monies are being wasted. Although your district will not have a tax levy on the ballot for another 3 years, the unremitting criticism will surely take a toll on your district's image if not dealt with. Your board president and superintendent reach agreement with the city manager and council chair to hold quarterly luncheon meetings of the two boards, along with top executives on both sides of the fence, explicitly to address questions and issues. In light of the stakes involved, you and your colleagues on the school board unanimously support taking 2 hours every 3 months for these luncheon sit-downs, and the board's community relations committee agrees to put together issue agendas for each meeting, in collaboration with the superintendent and director of public affairs.

So many stakeholders, so much at stake, so little time: obviously you and your school board colleagues must be highly selective in scheduling your hands-on, nongoverning involvement in stakeholder relations. As I have mentioned before, there will always be a clear and present danger of overextension and the dilution of your critical governing role, which is the preeminent mission of every school board. The best protection you have in this regard is to ensure that your board, preferably through a standing committee, reaches agreement with your superintendent on formal, detailed stakeholder relations strategies that are meticulously managed. Merely taking the still all-too-common squeaky-wheel approach (responding to the stakeholders who produce the loudest or most frequent squeaks) will put your district at risk of wasting precious time to produce modest results.

A WORD ON THE BOARD PRESIDENT AND SUPERINTENDENT

There is little confusion, in my experience, about the basic distinctions between the leadership roles of the school board president and superintendent. Your board president is essentially CEO of the board (certainly not the district), in this capacity being accountable for chairing full board meetings and playing a strong leadership role in developing your board's leadership capacity. By contrast, your district's superintendent is CEO of the whole district, in this capacity being accountable to your school board as a whole for all internal operations of your district, making sure it is well managed and that it achieves strategic and operational performance targets. There is universal agreement that the superintendent is accountable—and reports—only to the school board as a whole, never to the board president, who should not give direction to the superintendent (unless speaking for the whole board) or evaluate the superintendent's performance.

There is some potential for conflict, however, where external community relations are concerned, since this is shared turf, and both the board chair and superintendent are widely seen as preeminent spokespeople for the school district. Board presidents and superintendents have averted conflict by taking two simple steps:

1. Making sure their participation in external relations fits within the board's established structure and processes (e.g., working through the board standing committee responsible for overseeing community relations, rather than launching initiatives "outside the loop," and working closely with the district's public information officer).

2. Reaching detailed agreement—with the advice and counsel of your public information officer—on how to handle specific requests and questions that come directly to the board president or superintendent (e.g., to be interviewed on a particular issue by the reporter on the education beat for the local newspaper; to appear on a talk show; to return a telephone call asking for the district's official position on a matter). Superintendents who are truly board savvy, in my experience, whenever feasible defer to their board presidents when opportunities arise to speak on behalf of their districts.

AND GOING INSIDE

By virtue of your position as a school board member, you have a valuable role to play in building and maintaining a healthy internal climate inside your school district, but this is an area where you must tread warily and avoid abusing your influence. The fact is, your superintendent is preeminently responsible for all internal operations in your district, including the internal culture, and your hands-on internal involvement could easily impede the superintendent in playing his or her CEO leadership role. For example, there is always the clear and present danger that an administrator or faculty member will take advantage of direct interaction with you or one of your board colleagues by attempting to circumvent your superintendent, say, by questioning one of the superintendent's policies or actions or by attempting to lobby for an initiative your superintendent opposes.

The following well-tested guidelines will ensure that you and your board colleagues make an important internal contribution without risking any damage to your superintendent's CEO role:

- Carefully manage internal board member involvement, employing if feasible a standing committee to set priorities for—and to schedule—such involvement and to monitor the results.
- Make sure involvement utilizes board members in a symbolic and largely ceremonial internal role that clearly has nothing to do with day-to-day operations of the district. For example, it would clearly be inappropriate for you or one of your board colleagues to participate in an administrative staff meeting at which operational issues are being dealt with. By contrast, numerous opportunities exist for symbolic and ceremonial involvement that really will contribute to a healthier internal culture in your district:
  - Attending, and perhaps speaking at, the annual faculty convocation and district graduation ceremonies
  - Sitting at the head table at awards ceremonies, perhaps speaking and presenting awards
  - Supporting by your attendance musical, athletic, and other programs in your district
  - "Trooping the line" by visiting classrooms in the various buildings
  - Providing visible support to your superintendent when he or she is launching a major initiative—especially when significant internal resistance is likely—by, for example, joining the superintendent on the stage when he or she is announcing and explaining the initiative to assembled faculty and administrators

If you proceed carefully, according to clear guidelines, you can contribute to a healthier internal climate while also enriching your governing experience through such symbolic and ceremonial involvement, without jeopardizing your superintendent's position.

ABOUT THE AUTHOR

Doug Eadie is the founder and president of Doug Eadie & Company, based in Palm Harbor, Florida. Over the past 25 years, Doug has consulted with nearly five hundred public and nonprofit organizations, including many school districts, in the areas of board and chief executive leadership and of innovation and change management. Doug is the author of fifteen books on public and nonprofit leadership in addition to *Five Habits of High-Impact School Boards*, including *The Board-Savvy Superintendent* (with Paul Houston) and *Eight Keys to an Extraordinary Board–Superintendent Partnership*. The Council for the Advancement and Support of Education (CASE) selected Doug's *Extraordinary Board Leadership: The Seven Keys to High-Impact Governance* to receive its H. S. Warwick Research Award for 2002.

Before founding his consulting practice, Doug held a variety of public and nonprofit executive positions, including budget director of a large city and community college senior executive. He served as a Peace Corps volunteer for three years, teaching ancient history and English at the Tafari Makonnen Secondary School in Addis Ababa, Ethiopia. Doug is a Phi Beta Kappa graduate of the University of Illinois at Urbana and received his master of science in management degree from the Weatherhead School of Management at Case Western Reserve University.

Other Resources on Board Leadership and the Board–Superintendent Partnership

From NSBA

The National School Boards Association (NSBA), headquartered in Alexandria, Virginia, is the preeminent resource on public school governance. NSBA's *American School Board Journal* frequently addresses various facets of school board leadership, and its bimonthly newsletter, *Updating School Board Policies*, contains in-depth articles on a wide variety of current and provocative policy-related topics. In addition, NSBA offers for sale a wide range of publications, described at its website, www.NSBA.org.

Among the many books offered for sale by NSBA, I think that five are most pertinent to your work as a school board member. *The Key Work of School Boards Guidebook* (2000) provides a framework of eight key action areas that effective boards have focused on. *Team Leadership for Student Achievement: The Roles of the School Board and the Superintendent* (2001), by Ellen Henderson, Jeannie Henry, et al., addresses the leadership roles of board members and superintendents in the eight key action areas described in *The Key Work of School Boards Guidebook*. *Becoming a Better Board Member: A Guide to Effective School Board Service* (1996), by Kristen J. Amundson, Ellen Ficklen, et al., deals with a wide range of topics, such as school law, personnel, finance, curriculum, and public opinion. *Thinking Differently: Recommendations for 21st Century School Board/Superintendent Leadership, Governance, and Teamwork for High Student Achievement* (2000), by Richard H. Goodman and William G. Zimmerman Jr., covers a number of steps that the authors believe should be taken to develop and strengthen local school board–superintendent leadership. And Eugene R. Smoley Jr.'s *Effective School Boards: Strategies for Improving Board Performance* (1999) focuses on practical strategies that can be employed in strengthening school board leadership.

From ScarecrowEducation

Five Habits of High-Impact School Boards is the third book in ScarecrowEducation's trilogy on school board leadership and the board–superintendent partnership. The first two books, jointly published by ScarecrowEducation and the American Association of School Administrators (AASA), are *The Board-Savvy Superintendent* (2002), by Paul Houston and Doug Eadie, and *Eight Keys to an Extraordinary Board–Superintendent Partnership* (2003), by Doug Eadie. Two other Scarecrow books of interest to readers who want to deepen their understanding of the board–superintendent working partnership are *Roles and Relationships: School Boards and Superintendents* (1994) and Jack McCurdy's *Building Better Board/Administrator Relations: Problems and Solutions* (1993).